PARANORMAL
GLOUCESTER

PARANORMAL
GLOUCESTER

LYN CINDEREY

AMBERLEY

First published 2009

Amberley Publishing
Cirencester Road, Chalford,
Stroud, Gloucestershire, GL6 8PE

www.amberley-books.com

© Lyn Cinderey, 2009

British Library Cataloguing in Publication Data.
A catalogue record for this book is available from the British Library.

ISBN 978 1 84868 249 8

Typesetting and origination by Amberley Publishing
Printed in Great Britain

I would sincerely like to thank everyone that has contributed to helping me compile this book and for all the stories that have been told to me, and for stories I have read about this wonderful 'paranormal' and 'ghostly' historic city.

*All my friends, for me going on and on about my book.
My love to all of you.*

CONTENTS

FOREWORD

I first met Lyn back in the summer of 2004 when I was making radio features for the community radio station Stroud FM. This was my first paranormal investigation and I needed to find an experienced group to help me. I am delighted that Parasoc (The Myers Paranormal Society) took up the challenge as Lyn was then a member and after this first investigation we became very good friends. We continued to go on investigations together and I was pleased and honoured that she asked me to join her in conducting ghost walks around Gloucester. These tours soon became known as the Gloucester Ghost Walks. Everyone who has met Lyn will know how kind, generous and loving she is to all. It is amazing how many people, having just met her on her tours, soon become firm friends with her. I did the ghost walks with Lyn for about a year and I can definitely say that it is one of those very proud times that I have in my life. Although Lyn's walks from the start were brilliant she is constantly coming up with new ideas and ways of making the tours as enjoyable as possible for the public. As you know Lyn's walks are still going from strength to strength and generating a lot of media interest. She is often called upon by local radio and newspapers to comment on any paranormal activity. This forward has been written before I have had the chance to read the book, although I have seen the introduction. However, if it is anything like her tours I am sure this book will be wonderfully spooky and entertaining. I'd like also to take this opportunity to thank Lyn for being a wonderful and true friend.

Paul Goddard

ACKNOWLEDGEMENTS

I would like to thank all my friends and colleagues for all their support and their stories and pictures given to me freely to complete this book. Also, not just for the book but for their friendship, which to me is very important.

There are so very many of you to mention and I would be terrified if I listed you all and forgot someone, so all I can say is if I have talked to you, met you, got drunk with you (did I say that?), if our paths crossed in anyway, then it is YOU that I am referring to.

I dedicate this book to each and every one, you all know who you are.

A special thank you to Eileen Fry and Rosemary Harvey, authors of: *Ghost Trails of Gloucester's Past*, and *Haunted Gloucester*.

To Paul Soden, owner of the Café René and The Old Bell and of course not forgetting A. M.

To Ruth and David of The Cross Keys.

To Amanda and Ed from the Dick Whittington pub.

To Philip Moss, author of *Historic Gloucester*.

To Darrell Kirby, author of *The Story of Gloucester*.

To Steve and Jean of the Services Club.

PREFACE

LOVED ONES THAT HAVE PASSED ON

No end of people have told me of their own personal experiences of their loved ones that have passed on, including beloved pets that have come back to visit. I myself have heard two of my pets running up the stairs to my bedroom less than a month of them both passing. It was very comforting to hear this, and my husband also heard them at the same time.

While staying with a friend once she informed me that if I felt something jump up on my bed in the night, not to worry it was her cat that often comes back to visit. That night I woke up as I felt something walking around the bottom of my bed, then settle down by my feet, it was quite a lovely experience.

One night I was dreaming that I was with a large black dog we used to have and I was stroking him, I really felt like he was solid once more, and as I gradually woke up, I noticed my hand was still making the stroking movements at the side of the bed, but no dog was there.

A very dear friend of mine lost her beloved husband and soul mate, it was a very distressing time for her and all the family, I felt so useless and would have done anything I could to relieve their pain. I prayed so much for strength to be there for them all, especially for my dear friend. I stayed with her the night before the funeral and could not sleep very well, when I suddenly saw a strange light in one corner of the bedroom. I tried to think logically what this was, but could not explain it. I never forgot it and it will remain with me always, as I do feel it was my friend's husband watching over his beloved wife.

He also came to me in my own home in the form of an alarm call, I would lie in bed and suddenly I heard my mobile phone ringing, I went to answer it, and was startled to find it was not even turned on, but as I was awake now, thought I had better get up.

Another morning I heard the door bell go, I got up to answer it, and called out to my son, who was downstairs, who is at the door, ringing the bell, he said 'No one's there, and anyway we have not got a door bell . . .' 'Oh crikey' I said, 'No we haven't have we?'

I looked at the time, 11am exactly, the time that I had been previously woken up. My friend said she felt it was her husband telling me to get up and to look after his wife for him, to which I replied, I think you're right you know.

Another time, I could not sleep at all and at 3am decided to get up and go down into the kitchen for a drink, while I was down there I had this constant urge to write. 'Write what?' I was saying to myself. So much so that eventually I gave in and got a pen and paper and started writing, and writing, and writing, I could not stop, just as if someone was controlling my pen.

Then I stopped, quite exhausted, but not really realising what I had written. I looked at the time and I had been writing for two hours.

I showed my friend what I had written, and she was amazed and yet happy, she said that it was her husband's hand writing, and even his spelling mistakes, also, I had written things that only they knew about and no one else.

Wow was I spooked or what, but in a nice way. I had felt that I had fulfilled my duty and was delighted that I could help, in a way that I would NEVER EVER have envisaged.

INTRODUCTION

This is me in my Ghost Walk costume.

This is my first ever attempt at writing a book and I've been delighted to be given this opportunity. I hope you enjoy it.

There won't be very many big words, it's been written in a plain and basic way so that you can easily pick it up and put it down, or read it from beginning to end without getting tired. It is as honestly put together as I possibly can make it. There won't be a lot of history but there will be some, if the stories need it, because there are plenty of good books on that subject already (authors mentioned further on). Also I feel that if you wanted history then you would buy history books, not paranormal books. That's my excuse and I'm sticking to it!

The paranormal has always been a favourite subject of mine and apparently many more people too these days. With a lot of coverage on the TV and such like proving the point and a lot of people that I have met on my ghost walks have said how much they would love to know more, and go on overnight investigations.

TV, to a certain extent, has glorified the word paranormal but in all honesty it is not an easy subject to follow, things can get a little in-depth with some people, others see it as a bit of fun.

I personally wish to find out as much as I possibly can to see if there really is life after death and that we don't just die and nothing continues.

The stories told in this book are accounts of people told to me directly, I have researched, experienced myself or been told by friends and colleagues.

It is of course a matter of opinion whether you believe or not, we all have the right of free will, and I for one respect that. A lot of people that I have spoken to say that they will only truly believe if they see something for themselves, I can understand that fully. Also, a lot of people have said they do believe because of things that have personally happened to them. Such experiences I have had myself.

I was born in Gloucester in 1950. For some strange reason I cannot remember an awful lot of my early childhood until I was about eight years old.

Mum had TB in her early twenties and was in and out of Standish Hospital a lot and for long periods of time.

So my sister Maureen (Mo) and myself were in and out of children's homes and foster parents and staying with aunties and uncles.

Peter, our brother, was also ill a lot with lung and chest illnesses so he was staying at Oak Bank School in Stroud Road.

Dad was a lorry driver and had to use his spare time visiting us all, which must have been horrendous for him as we were all in different places. Dad died as a result of a hit and run accident.

My brother died of ill health at the age of only thirty-one years.

Mum died of ill health at Standish Hospital.

So that just left my sister Mo and myself as immediate family apart from cousins, aunties and uncles of course.

I met and married Tony in March 1968 and we have two sons Shaun born 1969 and Dean 1971.

As a mother and wife I did all the usual things but was still always missing my family and the tremendous gap that I couldn't seem to fill.

We had a few friends when we first got married and we had lots of parties in the house, I guess I was trying to compensate.

I had two nervous breakdowns in a space of fifteen years which looking back now I still wonder why I had to go through all that and sometimes cannot believe that I did get through it, but with the help of my dear sister Mo and my cousin Faye and friends and family I did. I suppose that was the start of realising how important friends and families are to us.

It wasn't until some years later that while working at a cash and carry warehouse in Gloucester that I realised the true meaning of friendship. I learnt an awful lot there about how to listen and talk to people and to help each other out when needed.

I started reading about dreams and their meanings because for a long time now I kept getting dreams, and sometimes the same ones. I bought a dream interpretation book and took it to work to read in our lunchtimes. It became a talking point and I suddenly realised how much people were interested in dreams, the paranormal, and the spiritual side of life.

We often sat at a table and discussed each other's dreams I became aware that in time I was able to analyse their dreams for them myself and only referred to the book afterwards to see if I had the same or close to the same analysis as in the book.

I can tell you at this stage the book became very well used and tatty.

At this time I was also seeing a counsellor as I suffered with depression and a nervous breakdown. Two years later I was a different person with a different outlook on life.

I received the nickname of "dream witch" from my work colleagues.

This name I used as my screen name when I first acquired a computer and still use it today.

'Where is this story leading?' I hear you ask.

Well . . . I believe this was the start of how I am now and what I have accomplished thus far.

My very first spiritual experience was one that will never ever leave me.

My Brother Pete

I was dreaming that I was with my brother Peter, who had passed away that year, he was a very proud man and was very often ill but would never moan about it, he just got on with his life the best he could.

The dream was so vivid, I was walking and talking with him and laughing, he looked so well and was full of life. We both had the same sense of humour and wit.

I told him how much I missed him and he said he will always be around. I was holding his hand and he said I have to go but don't worry I am fine now and happy. I did not want him to leave and as his hand was slowly slipping away from mine I could physically feel his hand. As I was slowly waking up I could still feel his hand leaving my hand. When I was fully awake, I sat bolt upright in bed and started to cry, but these were tears of joy. My husband asked me what was wrong, when I told him he said it was just a dream. I replied, 'Oh no, that was NOT just a dream, I WAS with Pete I know I was, it was real.' I was still crying but was very happy that Pete was with me even for such a short time, but I will never ever forget and no one can take that wonderful experience away from me.

You see . . . when Pete was ill and being rushed to Standish Hospital he stopped breathing on the way, so they had to rush him to Gloucester Royal where they immediately put him on a life support machine because he had stopped breathing for a while.

The machines were just pumping oxygen around his body and blowing him up like a balloon so I was told. His wife had to make the devastating decision to turn them off.

I was asked if I wanted to go and see Pete but declined as I wanted to remember him as he was.

So really I never got to say goodbye and this is what hurt the most. Afterwards I really regretted it but it was too late. In my heart of hearts I know that is why Pete returned and gave me the chance to say goodbye.

After this experience I have never worried about Pete again as I now know he lives on, in my heart, mind, and spirit.

God bless you Pete, my brother Pete.

Since then I have become more and more inquisitive with regard to the spiritual side of life.

I went to a Spiritualist church several times and found this to be very uplifting, sometimes I would get a message from the visiting medium and was often told I had a gift, and why was I always doubting myself? At first I thought 'No way not me!'

But over the years I have become very sensitive to other people's needs and have become a very positive person. Listening to my inner-self and intuition more, instead of ignoring it.

I still felt as if something was missing in my life and that there was something I needed to do.

After joining paranormal groups and going on investigations which I still love doing I found my thirst for more and more information of the history of my city was growing. Until such time that it came hand in hand with the ghost stories of Gloucester.

I read ghost stories from Eileen Fry and Rosemary Harvey's books which I found fascinating and found out that they used to run ghost walks in Gloucester many years ago.

I thought, wow I would love to do that, but didn't want to step on anyone's toes so to speak. I then found out that the two ladies did not run the ghost walks anymore and neither did anyone else. What a great shame I thought, as I realised how much potential there was in the city.

I have recently met Eileen Fry and Rosemary Harvey in 2008 we had a lovely chat and a cup of coffee. We talked about their experiences with the ghost walks. They were delighted that Paul and I had carried on where they left off so to speak and wished me well. They were two really delightful ladies, who I admire very much and I'd like to thank them for their support in writing this book.

PAUL AND MOIRA GODDARD AND MYSELF

So I along with my dear friend Paul Goddard we started our ghost walks in 2005. Moira Goddard another dear friend came along sometimes to and was an excellent prompter.

We did a lot of research first and worked out a route between us where to take people.

We did this together for approx a year and built up our ghost walks which became very popular with local people.

Paul then left to further his career in NLP and I'm very pleased to say that he passed the courses and is now a qualified practitioner of NLP.

I carried on alone for a while, sometimes with a friend or two that came with me now and again.

I now have two people that help me: David Baldwin and Shaun Moore. We do our best to make our ghost walks entertaining and educational.

While running the weekly ghost walks I have made numerous friends and colleagues, at long last filling the gap that I once longed for.

To the best of my knowledge the stories that are told to me and recounted here, are a true account of what people have experienced themselves or friends and families that have. Or indeed are what I have personally experienced myself, or read in local books on Gloucester.

PARANORMAL — WHAT DOES THIS WORD ACTUALLY MEAN TO MOST OF US?

Here are a few definitions of this word:

Beyond normal scientific explanation.

Not in accordance with scientific laws.

Paranormal phenomena are those supposedly due to powers of the mind that go beyond the normal.

GLOUCESTER'S GHOSTS

Gloucester is a very old and historic city going right back to Roman times and as a reader you would expect it has quite a few very interesting 'Ghost Stories'. This book tells you about some of the stories that have been told by local people in various locations around the city, past and present. Also what I have personally experienced myself.

'Is Gloucester that haunted?' people have asked me. In my opinion, the answer is yes, most definitely.

When I was at school many moons ago (now there's an old expression) I hated history, I thought it was boring.

Now I'm an adult and conduct The Gloucester Ghost Walks I cannot get enough history to add to my weekly walks and ghost stories.

People love to be spooked and love to be entertained especially when it is on their own doorstep.

To add history to it and for people to look up and around the city is a bonus for me, when they say, 'Wow! I never realised that', or 'I never knew that was here'. The expressions on their faces are a real picture to see.

So many people also say 'I used to work there when it was so and so shop or pub and there was something spooky about that place'.

Or 'When I was there I experienced something'. Hence the writing of this book entitled, *Paranormal Gloucester*.

A Gazetteer of Gloucester Hauntings

A.G. Meek Shoe Shop

This is a shoe shop in Westgate Street. The staff in the shop have had several unusual experiences happen in this shop for many years.

On an upper floor is a storeroom where they store all the new stock when it comes in, on several occasions the next day they have had to pick up all the new stock that had been neatly stacked as it is strewn all over the room. Just as if someone was having a real good look at it all. This has been associated with a spirit of a lady who wears a very strong old fashioned perfume like lilac or lavender. Maybe she lived in this building many years ago.

Another story is of their staff room, they neatly place clean cutlery on a cloth in the kitchen area to use when they have their meals at lunchtimes. Yet when they go into the kitchen sometimes the cutlery is missing and they know no one else has been in this room. This happens on a regular basis, they then go back later and the cutlery reappears and is neatly placed on the cloth again, the staff are very mystified at this. Is it the lady again?

There is also a story told many times of a little boy seen looking out of an upstairs attic window. He has been described as having short blonde hair, about seven to eight years old and holding his head in his hands looking very forlorn. Recently a medium said the little boy contacted him, and the boy told him that his name was David and he never had a surname because he was an orphan. He was made to climb the chimney to sweep it and he got stuck up the top, he tried to climb down but fell and hit his head on the floor and became unconscious. By the time he was found, he had died. The medium did say that David told him he was buried in an unmarked grave in a church yard near the shop, but he was happy now, especially as he has now been identified. Will we ever see little David again peering out of that window? Who knows? I will still tell the story

but am glad in one way if David is not seen again, as he said he was happy, so if he is happy then I certainly am for him.

I really don't know for sure if the story of the medium contacting David is real or not, as in many cases it is up to the individual and as I am not a medium and cannot really doubt this man, it is a nice but sad tale to tell. We all have to make our own minds up on these matters as always. That is why we were given the right to feel free.

The other theory is that the little boy may well have been one of the pin factory workers that was used in Gloucester or he may be a victim of one of the fires that burned down in Westgate Street many years ago.

I have been into the room where he has been seen at the window, it is totally empty and derelict, as are two other attic rooms. This room, however, is the only room in which I felt very sad and quite weepy. The staff at the shoe shop do not like going into this room for the same reason.

AGE CONCERN CHARITY SHOP

This shop was not having things go bump in the night but having things going missing all the time. My friend Gill is the manageress of the shop and as she knew I was very interested in this sort of thing, she asked me if I would come along one night to investigate. Well . . . that's like a red rag to a bull to me, of course I jumped at the chance.

My friend told us that many things kept going missing and she felt it was maybe the children. She used to shout out loud to them and say 'come on, put that paperwork back please, I need it'.

She went out the room for a while and when she returned the paperwork that went missing had returned right on top of her desk clearly for her to see.

When we did the investigation I was in an upstairs room when three of us saw a shadow of a lady on the wall, her hair was pulled back into a bun. We all thought it may have been the shadow of one of our colleagues who had her hairstyle like that and we made her walk up and down in the room to see if we could create the same shadow we saw. But no luck, as the shadow we had seen was much higher up on the wall, and our friend wasn't tall enough.

So who was this mystery lady, was she the one that moved things, and if so why?

At approximately 2.30am when we had decided to pack up all our equipment down in the shop area we all heard a loud slam of the door behind us all, two of our friends saw what they described as a lady running from behind the door out along the corridor towards a back door, they both described her as the same shadow that they had seen upstairs. I can tell you in all honesty, boy, did we jump when that door slammed!

We later did some research on this shop and found out that where we saw the lady run along the corridor was actually once an outside alley.

They had added the corridor and the back of the shop in later years. Maybe this lady was running outside and we were the intruders in her home. We may never know. Not unless we ever get invited back that is. In some cases like this it is great when we do get the chance to go back, to see if anything similar happens again.

ANGLIAN WINDOWS

In 1988 on Hallowe'en night, two men agreed to stay overnight in the haunted offices of Anglian Windows in Westgate Street, Gloucester, as part of a fund-raising scheme. Severn Sound radio had earlier installed equipment in a locked room so that the two could broadcast live on radio.

When they arrived for their vigil, they found the door still locked but inside the room all the radio equipment had been disturbed and wires pulled out. Bravely they went on with their plan and throughout the night recorded and broadcast a series of crashes and bangs, a table being turned over, lights being switched on and off.

Earlier that year, a lady who worked in the Anglian showroom, told the publication *Source* (August 11th, 1988) of how eight members of staff had all seen a carpet lift itself up as if there was someone underneath it, and a host of other unexplained incidents.

This was followed by the sighting of a robed man in the showroom and a hand basin being thrown down the stairs.

In September, medium Phillip Seff was called in and held a seance, attended by journalists and photographers.

During the seance, Seff made contact with a man with long white hair and a beard, wearing a grey robe, who had broken his neck and died after falling from the building.

One of the two men who spent the night in the building, café owner Steve Pugh, had had an earlier experience of the ghost, so he knew something of what to expect.

Working in his café he heard a crash and breaking glass from an upstairs window of the Anglian building. Inside, in a locked and bolted room, he and office manager Jean Brown discovered that a large wardrobe had mysteriously been pushed into a window, scattering glass into Bull Lane.

Seff held a second seance in the building just prior to the vigil, this time the 'monk like' person told him that he was searching for a key he'd lost there. After reading this story in the local paper and in Eileen Fry's book *Ghost Trails of Gloucester's Past*, I went into the shop that is now called The Phone Zone but the new owners declined to tell me anything. I wonder why? Had it all gone quiet, or did they not wish to disturb things? Will we ever know again what goes on in this shop? I for one will keep my eye on it.

ARCHDEACON SCHOOL

I have been told of this story by several different people but not so much in detail as recorded in Eileen Fry's book. My sincere thanks to her for this story.

The College of Technology annexe in Archdeacon Street, off Westgate Street, Gloucester, is a resource centre for teachers, but it was originally built in 1852 as a school.

During alterations in 1968, the decorators used the headmaster's office beneath the main stairs as a store-room. One morning when they unlocked the office, they were dumb-struck to discover that tins of paint had been mysteriously spilt.

The caretaker was hit by a shovel in the empty boiler room, lights were mysteriously turned on and the children began seeing an old man with white hair wearing a gown and mortar board, whom they christened Charlie.

Eventually the school called in J.A. Brooks, author of *Ghosts and Witches of the Cotswolds*, who held a seance at the school on Midsummer Night's Eve.

He successfully made contact with the ghost who told him that he had taught at the school a long time ago. In too much of a hurry he had run down the stairs, slipped and fatally injured himself. He was carried to the headmaster's study, the room in which the paint was spilled, and had died there.

The presence of the builders had upset him, he told the seance he had spilled the paint to frighten them. He hadn't, he said Brooks wanted to harm the caretaker but was just trying to pass the shovel.

When the alterations were completed, the master's ghost quietened down again, although there have been some occasional unexplained incidents in the building.

The Archdeacon School in Clare Street was known as the 'Ragged School' of the city. This was the school where children were able to leave their inadequate homes behind and begin to learn to read and do sums. A further tribute to the work begun by Robert Raikes.

The school in Clare Street soon became popular and even today some remember their schooldays there. The place is no longer a school and Donald Jones only knew the fine building when he went to repair a window at five o'clock one evening in 1979. Mr Jones used to work for Gloucestershire Council as a glazier and was keen to tell me what happened to him. He had a message to go to the former school in Clare Street as a window was broken and needed to be replaced as soon as possible. It was nearly time to pack up and go home but Mr Jones thought he could just about get the job done in time. He approached the front entrance and stepped inside the door, just a routine task to be completed quickly. The place was quiet and empty except for a man sitting on a chair. Donald asked the man where he could find the caretaker and the man obligingly pointed his finger to the direction of the stairs. Mr Jones found Marj the caretaker who was pleased to see him arrive so quickly. 'How did you know where to find me?' she asked. Donald replied that the man downstairs had shown him where to go. 'Oh you must have seen our ghost', replied Marj quite undisturbed, 'There is no one else in the building.' The caretaker went on to tell him that there were many unexplained things regularly taking place in the building. A schoolteacher who had been well-loved by the children in his care had one day accidently fallen down the stairs. He was helped into the headmaster's study which at that time was a small room close to the staircase. Before anything could be done to help the poor man he died. Since that time his ghost had been seen allegedly even by the children in a class. Marj said that lights had been seen to go on and off and toilet doors had been locked from the inside. Even local police had been called one night because of lights in the building. Nothing was found. Other staff had felt a push in the back.

ARGOS

This story is from a lady called Sue Butler who used to work in Argos when it was in Northgate Street. Probably in the early eighties where they used to go up stairs into the stock room on the third floor, where she said that the staff there believed there was a spirit there, they never saw it but could hear shuffling, and boxes would be moved or knocked on the floor. There was only ever one or two people in that area that were accounted for.

Sue said she had heard rumours that there was a spirit lady that the staff called Gladys, they used to call out to Gladys and say hello. She also said they were always hearing strange unexplained noises and believes that it is definitely haunted. She still wonders to this day if 'Gladys' is still there.

BEARLAND RESTAURANT

Sincere thanks again to Lorna.

This happened three years ago when my husband myself and two of our friends went out one September evening, our destination was Bearland the restaurant. The atmosphere was great and we had a lovely night. The restaurant was full, and our first course came, then over by the far wall as plain as day were two maids dressed in twisted wool grey-blue long dresses, with starched white aprons and cloth caps. They did not communicate so they were not spirit but ghost energies stuck in time.

I also have a friend who is psychic, who works in town. Since the extensive building work going on at the docks she has seen so much shifted activity that seems to just go anywhere, such as a surgeon performing a operation that was seen in Clarence Street. These shifted energies are a recurrence as the building work is still ongoing.

BELL WALK

By day, Gloucester's centre is busy with shoppers, and the Bell Walk precinct is at the very heart of this active city. Everything one could ask for can be be found in Bell Walk, which is a meeting place for old and young alike.

Bell Walk at night, though, is a very different place. The area is securely locked at both entrances, and only the security guards are allowed in to keep an eye on the wide variety of shops.

An assistant security manager there told of strange nocturnal occurrences that were reported to him and for which he could give no explanation.

An Alsatian guard dog called Bruce was regularly used on the Bell Walk beat. He was a good dog, and afraid of nothing. Nothing, that is, except walking towards the Southgate Street end of Bell Walk. His fur would stand on end, and he would rigidly refuse to go any further. It's possible that he had sensed something strange there, but whatever the reason, he would never venture to that part of the precinct.

One night two workmen came to repair the escalator in Bell Walk. It had been decided that it would be easier for them to do the job when the precinct was closed, so that they would not cause any inconvenience to shoppers.

The men arrived from Bristol with all the equipment they needed for their task, and began work for the night. They left their tools nearby, in a large metal container which they had locked up. When they had been working for some time, they found that they needed a tool from the container, which, to their astonishment, lay open and unlocked. They got the tool, locked the box and resumed work, puzzled as to how it came to be open.

Some time later, they returned to the box. Once again it was unlocked, the open lid gently swinging to and fro. None of its contents were missing, and no one else was anywhere on the premises. This happened three times, and eventually the men were so troubled by the feeling that something or someone was around them that they packed up their tools, left the precinct and refused to finish the job at night. During the day when they carried on the work, they experienced no trouble.

Two security guards, working at night, were watching the closed circuit television screen from a room above the precinct. Suddenly, there appeared on the screen the mysterious shadow of a figure walking along the floor from the escalators along to the entrance of Woolworths (now closed). The two men dashed down the stairs, expecting a confrontation with an intruder, but the whole place was silent and empty. There was no possible way out, and certainly nowhere to hide; it was a complete mystery. Oddly enough, it was the same area which Bruce, the fearless guard dog, had been afraid of.

BERKELEY STREET

This story is from Keren.

I am based at Berkeley Street where we have 21 flats in No 16, 18 and 20. We have also had some ghostly activity here which you may be interested in. A mysterious grey shape of a person seen in No 16 hallway on CCTV which did not move, a fridge being turned

off and a dog growling at something in the room in flat 3/16. It was cold in flat 18F even though the radiator was on and doors were slamming shut.

THE BLACK AND WHITE FISH AND CHIP SHOP

This lovely old building is over 500 years old, situated in Longsmith Street, which is a very old part of the city. The shop used to be a private dwelling, but is now a fish and chip restaurant.

In 1995 it is recorded that four visitors from our city decided to eat here for lunch. They needed a rest after looking around the city and became rather hungry as do many visitors and tourists that come here. They sat down in the upper floors, which is the restaurant area, probably remarking on the somewhat uneven floor as I have many times when I have been in there myself.

After lunch they wanted to carry on exploring the city and the ladies said they wanted to visit the toilet before setting off. The friends went to use the toilet but saw a lady in grey disappear into the room. They waited and waited for her to come out. They became very anxious. They wondered what on earth could have happened to the lady, even suggesting that perhaps she had died in there. They called the waitress, who went upstairs to investigate, but no one was there.

The ladies were convinced that they had seen someone go in the room and that no one had come out. The staff were unable to convince them that they had seen a ghost, for they too have experienced ghostly goings on for many years in the place. The then owner says he has heard doors banging when the place was empty and his wife says she too has seen someone running upstairs though she later found no one in the place. The present owners have said they feel as if someone is walking around in the upper rooms even though they know no one is there.

BLACKFRIARS PRIORY

MONK IN PRAYER

In the remains of the Dominican priory of Blackfriars in 1870, one Alice Godfrey saw the ghostly figure of a monk in prayer.

As she stared at the apparition she saw that he had fixed staring eyes and a grey lined face.

Almost 100 years later during restoration work, the skull of a man presumed to be a friar who died from a head wound, was unearthed in the church nave.

That same year a workman on a beam over the nave saw the ghost of a monk, one of his colleagues saw a friar with blood pouring out of his head running from the nave.

There is a story told that up to 250 bodies were found buried underground opposite the Priory which is now a car park. Beware where you park as you may just see something that you don't want to see, or even believe what you are seeing.

The once-thriving community became destitute. The last three monks were deliberately left to die of starvation as an example. No one was allowed to feed them or minister to them in any way. They died a horrible death. We also wonder at the fate of the people who had depended on their skills in healing the sick and feeding the poor. There was no place to turn to.

The church within the abbey settlement was large and impressive. Work began in 1960 to restore this fine surviving example of a Dominican abbey.

In January 1969 the local newspaper, *The Citizen*, gave prominent coverage to a surprising story about the 'Blackfriars ghost'. Restoration work was being carried out and many exciting finds were made. The foreman at this time was Bill Drew. His photograph appeared holding a skull belonging to a Black Friar, which had been discovered during the excavations. It had been buried in the floor of the church nave. The top of the skull had been neatly sliced across with a sharp instrument, obviously the cause of a violent death.

Strangely enough, a workman on the site had claimed to have seen the apparition of a friar running from the church with blood pouring from his head. At another time a friar — possibly the same one — had apparently been seen standing by the church door.

Another workman, Gary Lane, was working on a beam in the rewe of the church when he looked up and saw a monk standing just next to him – the figure then disappeared. Gary knew he was working alone, and no one else could have followed him. He was for a while unable to continue his work.

Gary was not the only workman to report strange sightings; the figure of a monk bent in prayer was also spoken of. The now restored kitchen was also quite a busy area, ghost wise. Some men even resigned from the job because of the ghostly company.

John Carroll, who worked at the abbey as a custodian, claimed that whilst he was sitting at his desk he became quite accustomed to the sound of heavy footsteps coming from the floor above.

In July 1539 the whole place was sold to a Sir Thomas Bell and his wife Joan. The deconsecrated buildings became a busy clothing factory, and the lovely church was converted into a private home. The house was called Bell's House. While the abbey thus became out of bounds to the public, at least this prevented the previous home of the Black Friars from being destroyed.

Monks are said to haunt this priory, and doors are known to have locked by themselves, and during 1969, when restoration was taking place a unknown cellar was discovered and the skeleton of a young child was found. A particular monk who wears a black robe is said to be seen near this place on many occasions and it is thought, there might be some link to the child.

BOOKENDS BOOK SHOP, WESTGATE STREET

What a fantastic sixteenth-century building this is, with many 'ghostly' stories that have been told over the past and even present-day.

At the very back of the shop which they call the shed they sell second-hand books. This has been a particular area where not one but two ghosts have been seen, one is of a young man probably in his teenage years, described as tall, slim, with short dark hair and always holding an open book in his hands, as if he is reading it as he is walking round. When he has been approached or spoken to by staff or customers he has never spoken or even looked at them, just as if he doesn't see or hear them.

Some very sensitive people have actually seen him disappear through the bookshelves. This young man does this on a regular basis, but always at the very back of the shop.

Another story is of an elderly lady, dressed in a rather old-fashioned manner, wandering around the very end of the bookshop, almost where the young man has been seen. She appears around closing time say the present-day staff. When they lock up, they go to look for the lady to tell her they are closing but she is nowhere to be found, and the staff say she did not pass them and leave the building. This occurrence also happens quite frequently.

Another strange thing always happens to the staff, when they are tidying up the books in the middle of the shop just opposite the door to upstairs they often see a shadow of what appears to be a young man running passed them into the doorway and up the stairs, but when they go up to see if he needs assistance no one is up there.

On one of my overnight investigations in this building (that once housed a judge and was once Colonel Massey's headquarters in the civil war of Gloucester) I, along with some colleagues of mine, encountered a very strange and rather unexplained experience on one of the upper floors. We had been investigating one of the front rooms that looked onto Westgate Street, it was not that dark as a very bright spotlight from a building across the road was shining in.

Around 2.30am after we had taken many pictures I said to my colleagues that this room was not active and asked if we should move on to another room. We all decided that was what we would do so we collected all our gear and went to move on.

We all had the shock of our lives when suddenly some books that had been standing up in a window sill suddenly flew off the sill and fell in front of my feet and even more spooky was that they landed in the same position that they had been on the window sill. Everyone in the room had witnessed this but not one person had filmed it as we were all preparing to move on, I consider this one of the times that I was well and truly told off by the 'spirits'.

Someone asked me once when I was telling this story on my ghost walks, 'did you look to see what the books were about?' Do you know what, I never even thought of that as I was very shocked, but I will always regret that now, as it may well have been of some significance or a clue to who, or what, was with us that night. I also remember going up stairs in a derelict part of the building and myself and a friend both heard the sound of typing on an old fashioned typewriter in a small room. We hesitated a while to go and take a look, but our curiosity got the better of us so we did look into the room. There was no one in there at all and no typewriter of any description. On one of our overnight investigations here, six of us went down into the basement area of the shop, past the area where the public are not allowed. It was very dark down there and quite dusty. The area had seperate alcoves, which made it even more spooky. We took pictures and filmed with our camcorders and did temperature readings, all the usual things we do. Then we decided to all sit in a tiny room at the end of one of the corridors.

This room had a doorway but no door attached, a colleague sat by this doorway and I sat next to her with the others next to me, snuggled up together in this tiny room.

We decided to keep quiet for a while and see if anything would happen. We didn't have to wait long before we heard a strange noise coming from the areas that we had all previously been.

The sound got closer and louder and we realised it sounded like something or someone being dragged along the floor, something very heavy.

By this time we were all frozen to our seats and even more snuggled up to each other as we continued to listen.

Suddenly, the sound got really loud and then stopped as if right outside the doorway next to my friend.

She screamed out, jumped onto my lap and would not move.

Of course her scream had a knock on effect for the rest of us and most of us screamed or yelled out in horror.

We then composed ourselves, had a good laugh at how brave we all were (not) and decided to go and take a look at where this sound had come from.

We looked everywhere, took more pictures yet saw nothing. Nor did we hear anything out of the ordinary.

Some time later I was doing some research into that building and around that area, and was told that a woman had been murdered under these tunnels by a monk.

Was this true? Was what we heard the monk dragging the body of the woman? Why did the sound of dragging abruptly stop right outside the doorway where we were sitting?

Will we ever know?

Bull Lane

This lane is a very interesting and historic lane. It got its name from The Bull Inn that sadly has long since gone. Before that it was called Gore Lane.

Along this lane an apparition has been seen of a man running and screaming holding his hand to his head which has blood pouring from it. The story told is that this man was assaulted and murdered by two men from The Bull Inn when he supposedly upset one of the women that used to regularly 'entertain' the gentlemen at this inn.

A very small building (still trading today) was once a butcher's shop along with many butcher's and slaughter houses along this lane. It was converted into a wine bar called Poets' Wine Bar (now called The Loft). The previous landlords, Mouse and Sarah, had been experiencing some really odd things happening in the building, such as hearing piano music playing yet there was no piano in the building or next door.

One night while Mouse was serving a customer at the bar, he noticed on the CCTV camera monitor that a dark figure was sat in a crouched position in a chair in the lounge area upstairs. He never saw this person come in, so he went up the stairs to see who it was. When he went into the room and looked at where he had seen the figure no one was there, or anywhere in the room, nor had anyone passed him on the stairs, which was the only way up to the room. He thought this very odd indeed as he knew what he had seen, so he went back downstairs and checked the CCTV camera's video tape, but to his annoyance and frustration there was no tape in the machine.

Mouse decided that this needed further investigation and asked myself and some friends from a paranormal group based in Cheltenham called Parasoc if we would look into this for him. Well, this was something we jumped at the chance to do and we of course said yes. So as soon as we arranged a date and time that we were all available we went along all geared up, with EMF (Electronic Magnetic Field) meters, voice recorders, cameras and camcorders, temperature readers, etc. We looked like we were moving in with all our boxes. There were six of us in all, and we went straight upstairs to start our investigation. Immediately Ross, our regular Medium, said that as he approached a certain chair in the lounge that he knew people had seen a dark figure sat there, not knowing any history or stories previously told. I found this amazing and thought, wow, looks like we are in for a good night.

We were not disappointed. We also found a very high EMF reading around the old fireplace, yet there was no indication that there was any electricity there. We also captured what we term as 'orbs'. These orbs are deemed to be the very first manifestation of a ghost.

Around 2.30am we decided we might call it a night and were just going to pack away all our equipment, when there was a very loud noise. We all looked straight at the same

area where there was a sash window, the others said that it sounded like someone had just slammed the window shut followed by two seperate thuds as if something had fallen on the floor, yet as we spoke about it and tried to re-construct the same sound it was not the same. Then we realised that when we first came upstairs earlier in the evening, all the windows were already shut. No one had opened them the entire evening. When we tried to open the window it was very hard to open and was stiff from not being used. But then I said, "Ok what about the two thuds we heard after the loud slamming sound, what was that?"

No one had any ideas, except to look at the camera footage that had been filming in the room, we had in fact four cameras one in each of the corner of the room. No evidence was filmed of anything moving, but we did record the sounds.

I did some research into the building and discovered it used to be a butcher's shop, I suddenly went all cold and visualised what the sounds we had heard were. My colleagues laughed and still don't agree with me, but see what you think.

Remember the old wooden butcher's blocks that they used to chop the meat on? And then the large cleavers? Well to me it sounded like the first loud slam was of these cleavers coming down onto the chopping block as if to chop of the head of a carcus, then followed by two thuds which would have been the head rolling off the block and onto the floor. Much more spooky than a window slamming don't you think?

Sometime later, I learnt that a murder had taken place in that building and an axe was used!

Make of that what you will.

In 2007 a man told me that he lived in one of the top floor flats in the building next to the loft and for a month or more he was woken up by footsteps pacing up and down the alley, every night after midnight he heard this, yet when he looked out of his window, no one was in site. Opposite his flat in the alley is a very old derilict building, I am fasinated with this building and can only find out so far that it used to be a clinic, what kind of clinic I have no idea yet, but will continue with my research and hope that one day I will find out. The man in the top floor flat said his side window looks directly into an upper window of his derilict building and welcomed me and a few friends to go there one night to see if we could see anything happen, as yet we have not done so. Maybe one day soon, but I really want to go inside the building rather than look through a window. Spooky I know, but that's me!

BULL LANE AND MARY PALMER (COURTESY OF EILEEN FRY)

In the sixteenth century there once stood a pub called The Bull Inn. The landlord was Ernest Daniel Tandy.

This notorious street was once known for the sad story of Mary Palmer of Littledean. Mary had come from her country home in the Forest of Dean to work for a spinster lady, Miss Eleanor Blunt. Apparently Miss Blunt was a formidable person demanding every penny to be accounted for and all time to be well spent.

Whilst in her services Mary met a local young man called Henry Sims who worked in Westgate Street. The young couple saw each other whenever they could snatch a moment, and soon began making plans for their future together. They were hoping to marry as soon as they had saved enough money, but as Miss Blunt disapproved they were forced to meet in secret.

In the Westgate Street shop where Henry worked there was a rival girlfriend named Miss Jones. She was hoping Henry would notice her and was extremely jealous when his attentions fixed on Mary.

On 19 September 1741 a terrible storm raged over the city. Thunder, lightning and heavy rain flooded down. Gales were all over the county. In the city the roofs fell in and chimney stacks collapsed into the streets below. Skies were black, thunderous and menacing, and everyone scurried for the shelter of their homes. It was on this very night that the life of Miss Blunt came to a violent conclusion.

The light of dawn eventually came and the bloodied body of poor Miss Blunt was discovered in her bed. The police were sent for and they made every effort to track down the murderer. During the course of their investigations they were bothered by the discovery that Miss Blunt's door was still locked from the inside. The handle of Mary Palmer's door also had bloodstains on it.

The envious Miss Jones immediately came to the conclusion that Mary had killed the old lady for her money so that she could marry Henry. She was happy to testify how she had heard the two sweethearts discussing their desperate need for £50, exactly the amount Miss Blunt had left Mary in her will.

Naturally Mary pleaded her innocence, but the circumstantial evidence weighed heavily against her. In spite of her protests and the cries of support from Henry, poor Mary was hanged in Gloucester jail, and her body buried within the walls. Henry was heartbroken. He knew his Mary could newer do such a terrible thing.

A few years' later two robbers were caught in Cirencester. They had been responsible for many crimes and one of them was given the death penalty for his misdeeds. Before his execution he gave a special request to meet the Governor of the jail.

During his talk with the Governor, prior to his hanging, he confessed that he and his accomplice had murdered Miss Blunt. He told how, taking advantage of the stormy weather and the deserted lane, the men had worked out a plan to climb across to the house of Miss Blunt from the building opposite. The street was very narrow then and the houses close together. A lot of people knew the old lady had hidden her money somewhere in the house, so they made a quick search after the murder. Then they returned to the house opposite leaving the room still locked from the inside.

This confession was announced and caused an uproar. Everyone knew that Mary had gone to her grave protesting her innocence. Mary's remains were removed from the prison and she was given a Christian burial. Henry led the funeral procession. This was a civic event and many people turned out to pay their respects. A tombstone was erected in memory of the innocent young girl, the girl Henry should have married. Miss Jones was hounded out of the city. A tragic miscarriage of justice indeed.

Many people will still remember Steve Pugh. His wife had a popular hairdressing business in Bull Lane. Robin Ledbury was also a hairdresser here and a friend of the Pugh's. Steve Pugh ran a very nice little café in the lane during the late 1980s. It was a very convenient spot for local folk and tourists as they were able to pop in for a cup of coffee or a tasty snack. It took over two storeys and was always busy. Bright check curtains were at the windows and in good weather there were tables out

Just inside the downstairs room on the wall hung a picture of an old lady in a rocking chair. The story behind the picture was this: one day Steve was in the room serving customers with nothing untoward happening when to his astonishment he saw the image of an old lady. She was dressed in old-fashioned clothes and was wearing a shawl around her shoulders. She was sitting in a wooden rocking chair which appeared to be rocking to and fro. The next minute the scene had disappeared. Was this anything to do with the Mary Palmer story? Perhaps Miss Blunt was checking on the customers. This experience made such an impression on Steve that he commissioned a painting to be exhibited downstairs.

After reading this story I have to say I had goose bumps all down my arms as I suddenly thought, is this the same building as the one we investigated and was the figure Mouse saw the same Lady in the upper room of Poet's Wine Bar, now called The Loft?

CAFÉ RENÉ LE PUB AND RESTAURANT

Previously this was called Greyfriars Inn. See 'Greyfriars'.

This is one of my favourite 'Haunts' – pardon the pun.

You will find this historic public house just off Southgate Street underneath an archway called Marylone Way, right next to St Mary De Crypt church and the historic Crypt School.

So many things have been seen, heard, felt, and indeed have happened in this place that it would take a whole book to detail every occurance. But here are the best and my most memorable to date.

The staff here have seen a figure of a cavalier walking past the serving hatch at the end of the bar in the early hours of the morning, they have also seen a woman walking through the restaurant who dissappears as she gets to the 600-year-old well that is situated just inside the front entrance, but this wasn't always the entrance. The well is actually outside, over the years builders have extended the pub and built around the well making it look like it was inside. Maybe this is why people have seen ghostly figures walking by the well as they would have actually been once walking in a courtyard.

They have also witnessed the measuring jugs that they measure spirits with jumping off the actual bottles, and even jiggling on the bottles as if someone is playing with them.

Bottles have fallen on the floor for no apparent reason, as have glasses. My friend Paul Goddard heard wispering and recorded voices seemly saying 'he's coming, Victor' up in the bar area leading down to the cellar.

On overnight investigations here we have caught several light anomilies or 'orbs' as they are termed. These lights are supposed to be energy forming from a spirit person trying to manifest into a full apparition. They get their energies from either us, or electric lights in the building or even from batteries in torches that very often drain of energy even though we know they were new batteries before we started. The pictures you see are some of the type of orbs we capture.

My cousin Faye Elliott and two other ladies were standing in semi-darkness just chatting, when all three of them saw a strange light come from the floor right in front of them which dissappeared directly into the wall.

They were pretty shaken up and very shocked as they told me that it seemed as if it came from nowhere and made a strange whooshing noise as it went by them.

My cousin Faye was a sceptic, but she said after seeing and hearing that, she now believes that something is definetly happening that is unexplained so far and is now totally convinced something 'paranormal' happened that night. They did not take any pictures nor did they have a torch on or were they using a camcorder at the time, and it was only those three in the area.

My cousin, since her experience at the René, has encountered another strange unexplained incident where she lives.

She lives at Sulgrave Close in an bungalow on the Grange Estate, Tuffley. Several times when she has been sat in her living room just watching TV, she has seen a dark figure walk from her bathroom towards her bedroom. She has a glass door, and can clearly see into her hallway where the bathroom is and her bedroom door, she cannot explain this.

I was with her one night, sat in her living room, and she was sat in her usual place when I myself twice saw a dark figure go from the bathroom across the hallway and into her bedroom. I never said anything to Faye the first time I saw it because I didn't

want to worry her as she lives there alone, but the second time I saw it, she saw me looking strangely at the glass door, and said to me "What's up, what are you looking at?" I told her what I had seen, and she smiled and said, "I'm so glad you saw that, because I have seen that many times while sat here and wondered if it was just me and my imagination." She had not previously told me anything and I was quite surprised that she had seen it too, but had not told me.

In the cellar bar just by the toilets a friend of mine named Tony was enjoying a drink and the music when he needed the loo. As he walked past some stairs he saw this young lady sprawled out on the stairs, apparently looking the worse for wear, so Tony asked her if she was ok. She never looked up or acknowledged him so he went on his way to the loo and as he looked round just double checking, she was gone, completely disappeared. He said there was no way that in a split-second she could have gone. He was a little shaken up, and refused to go down into the cellar bar for quite a while afterwards.

Paul Soden, the owner of Café René, had a very frightening experience one night. He told me that he had sent everyone home after pub hours and he knew he was the only person in the building. He was taking the till tray with the night's takings up to the office, but as he reached the door leading up to the stairs that led to the office he felt a hand in his pocket. He froze and says it felt very physical and felt like a man's hand. He was so frightened he dropped the till tray and ran up the stairs into his flat and got into bed and stayed under the duvet until morning. When the morning light came and he was brave enough to walk down the stairs, not expecting to find the money still there, he was most surprised to find the till tray and all the money still there on the floor where he dropped it.

When Paul first told me this story I had to admit I laughed and said to Paul that ghosts don't need money but if it had been a human person that money would not have been there.

He has heard horses and carts on cobbled stones just outside his bedroom window at around 6am on a regular basis yet when he looks out the window it is all quiet and no one is around.

The very same area is just outside the ladies toilets where several people including myself have felt as if being watched or followed by an unseen presence, some ladies will not even go in there on their own. On researching this area, we found out that this was once also part of the outside courtyard, added on to accomodate the toilets.

In an area down past the cellar bar the management and staff call a very large underground room and tunnel termed Deep Six. Walking right to the very end of this large, wide room is a wall and behind this wall is Eastgate shopping centre, this area is very dark and many people do not like this area as they have seen shadows and shapes around the wall, and even heard sounds of monks chanting.

On an overnight investigation down in Deep Six myself and several other people heard a very deep sigh of what sounded like a man's voice. When asking out loud if a spirit person was with us, we were all quite shocked at this response but also very excited. We also heard someone whistling and yet we were all accounted for and it was not any of us sighing or whistling.

Four men and two women did a seance around this area several years ago and it was abruptly stopped as the four men complained of pains in their chests.

In another area down in Deep Six there are what I describe as stone cubicles with letters and numbers on them W1 to W28. I found out that these 'cubicles' were used in the Second World War to house important documents and also used as a bunker.

In my research I found out that this may have also been used to administer to the plague victims in 1604 by the Greyfriars monks. Ruins of their abbey are very close by.

Is this why we have heard monks' chanting? On one of my ghost walks in 2006 four ladies told me that they used to work here, it was not called the Café René then, but the Greyfriars Inn. They were shocked when I took them around this area as they said the recent walls that are there now were tunnels that led underneath St Mary de Crypt church and the churchyard. They also recall not liking this area at all.

Several orbs have been caught around this area particulary by the far wall that behind was once buildings, a large orchard, and gardens.

People have gone up some stairs in this area that are within the shell of a building called Addison's Folly only to come back down rather quickly saying they felt ill or very sick.

Is this the area once used to help those poor victims dying of the plague?

The restaurant area is where a lady has been seen and a cavalier.

Sunday 25th January 2009 I went down into Deep Six underneath the pub with two friends Michala and David I was showing around. As we got to the stairs that lead into the shell of Addison's Folly my torch battery started to flicker on and off, at the very same time that David had heard a 'sigh' at the top of the stairs. I called out if any spirits were there with us and asked, if there was, would they affect my torch and make it brighter, as it was very dark down there and we couldn't see a thing in front of us. The torch suddenly became very bright indeed, to which myself and Michala said 'wow, thank you'.

Now can you please be very kind and turn it off, so we can varify that it is you that did that, whoever you are.

The torch suddenly went off, and would not come back on, I was flicking the switch on and off, but it would not come back on. David's camcorder then started to play up, and he had fully charged it. It was indicating that it was running out, yet he knew it had indicated a few minutes before that there was thirty minutes filming time left.

We moved on from this area back into the cellar bar, where David's camera was working again, and I looked on the seat where I had left the torch while I locked the door to deep six and it was on and a bright beam.

This kind of thing is always happening in various venues that I have been in, but never more so than the Café René.

Cemetery of St. Mary De Crypt church and the old Crypt School room, to the right of the picture is Café René which is situated next to Addison's Folly

Further reading on this historical inn, taken from the *Gloucester Citizen*, on November 15th 1988:

Burly builder flees from spooks — down at the pub

A GHOST at a Gloucester Inn which scared a burly 39-year-old builder so much that he took refuge overnight in a graveyard, is set to star in a book about the City's most haunted places.

And last week Geoffrey Lovatt from Oxford returned to the scene of his terrifying experience to meet two local women who have made it their business to investigate ghosts.

He and his partner Graham Kahl were renovating the eighteenth-century coach house in Southgate Street, now the Greyfriars Inn, when the work forced them to spend three nights in the building. That was when their problems began.

"I wasn't happy there even in daylight — I got nervous about the unexplained bumps and noises that were coming from upstairs," said Geoffrey. "Nights are cold and we couldn't see any alternative but to sleep in the building — the atmosphere was spooky, the noises got worse and doors were cracking eerily. "But the final straw was the second evening when I went to shut the outside gate only to see a wheelbarrow thundering towards me even though the courtyard was deserted.

"I told Graham I couldn't take any more and went and slept in my van in the graveyard opposite. I thought the dead would be a better bet than whatever was about at the Greyfriars Inn."

Gloucester ghost-hunting duo Eileen Fry and Rosemary Harvey came across the inn and the builders, while delving around Gloucester for stories for their book.

"It was no coincidence that we went onto that building site — you invariably find that ghosts are disturbed by renovation works, and this was a big one," said Mrs. Fry of Oxstalls Lane.

The pair heard tales of doors opening and closing in empty rooms, a light fitment on the wall was spinning round by itself.

More recently the Inn's manager, Keith Taylor, has heard machines playing even though they have not been plugged in.

Meanwhile Eileen and Rosemary have added the inn to their long list of haunted buildings in Gloucester for a book published in the spring of 2004.

Sometimes, extra spoons appear on tables, having been mysteriously moved from other settings. And yes, true to the form of whatever haunts the Greyfriars Inn, the lights still go on and off by themselves.

The inn is certainly an eerie place to visit. Perhaps, if you go there, you will find that out for yourself. If you dare.

For those wondering what Addison's Folly is here is a brief history of it:

Addison's Folly was built in 1864 by Thomas Fenn Addison in memory of Robert Raikes who, together with Thomas Stock (both pioneers of the Sunday school Movement) in 1780 started a Sunday school to teach poor children to read.

Addison's Folly

CASS-STEVENS INSURANCE, SPA ROAD

This is a very interesting building in Spa Road, Gloucester where I was asked to do a 'paranormal' overnight investigation because several staff that work here have experienced several unexplained phenomena.

I went to see them to discuss my public liability insurance for my weekly ghost walks, and while I was there, was asked if I would mind looking around the building and upper floors.

Of course I said yes, but added that I was not a medium and not to expect anything from me. But as I have learned over the years you never know what may occur.

I was shown around by a lady and a gentleman. I knew nothing of the building and its history and this was the first time I had been here.

To my surprise and shock I started picking up things that my mind's eye could see. At first I was very dubious to say anything for fear of being wrong and them thinking that I was some crazy woman.

But once I got started so much was going on in my head I could not stop. The main office, where I first sat down to discuss my insurance, was the first thing they asked me about, and did I feel anything here?

I said yes, in the far corner of the room a man has been seen walking through the wall across the room and into the far wall, but I added that there was once a door there. They looked at me and said "Yes, you are correct."

I was flabbergasted but very excited. We then went into some other rooms and corridors where again I reeled off information to them that I had no idea where it all came from.

In a staff room which was in the basement of the building I said that some people may have heard clicking noises in here or sounds of someone moving about, yet no one was in there when they looked.

The lady told me that one gentleman hated it down in this room and refused to go in there.

On an upper landing was an arch-shaped window. I said a lady in a long dress has been seen standing there looking out the window onto lovely gardens. They looked at each other in amazment and said "Yes, she had been seen also. There used to be a lovely garden outside but it is now a car park."

On the same landing we went into a room and I immediately saw a elderly lady sat on a sofa either knitting or crocheting, I could not quite make out which, and all the furniture in this room had a lovely cottage style look to it.

It looked very cosy and I felt that this was her living room where she too liked looking out of her window, but it wasn't the same lady I saw on the landing. I was told that this was indeed an elderly lady's living room and she did like to look out the window onto the lovely garden below, in fact she was the owner of the building.

In an upper level there were rooms not used now, only to store odd bits of furniture and boxes, we sat down in here for a while and called out asking if any 'spirit' person was with us. Although we never had any audible response we did capture some 'orbs' pictured below.

Chapter House

The Chapter House is partly built from stone used by the Romans who made Gloucester their home for 350 years. A section of the building was built by Bishop Alfred, somewhere between 1058 and 1066, just before poor King Harold was killed on his birthday at the battle of Hastings, and it was on this site that King William the Conqueror discussed the writing of the Domesday Book which was compiled in 1086.

The architecture of all but the eastern end of the cathedral is Norman. Edward the Confessor, the last Saxon king liked everything that was Norman. He even sent to France for builders to erect Westminster Cathedral, and to please him Bishop Alfred did likewise in Gloucester. Inscriptions in Lombardie on each side of the Chapter House commemorate distinguished Normans buried there in the eleventh and twelfth centuries, and when the floor was levelled in 1880, coffins were discovered beneath it. On the lid of one was written De Cadurcis. It was placed in the crypt of the cathedral.

Norman, a gentleman whose family have lived in Gloucester for many years, told the story his father told him when he was a boy. His father claimed that the Chapter House had a regular ghostly visitor from days gone by. It was said that the ghost appeared to walk across the room on his knees. They were mystified by this until it was realised that he must have been around in the days before the alterations to the floor, and was still walking on the previous surface, which was lower. Perhaps he would have preferred the place to have been left as it was, but of course we shall never know.

COACH AND HORSES

Back in 1997, Tony Lewis, landlord of the Coach and Horses in Gloucester, complained to the *Western Daily Press* about the ghosts that plagued his pub.

Only eight weeks after Mr Lewis, his wife Rosalind and three young children moved into the pub, they'd had enough of the bumps, bangs and apparitions that plagued them there.

Mr Lewis' son Carl, eleven, described a little girl wearing an old-fashioned dress and white pantaloons and the family was too scared even to sleep upstairs any more. And checking out the pub's history, Mr Lewis found that none of the previous landlords had hung around very long – there had been twenty in as many years!

We did an investigation in this pub around 2006 and we felt very, very uneasy in one of the upper bedrooms, I could not put my finger on exactly what it was, but I did not like it at all. I was due to stay the night there, but felt as if I did I would regret it and the feeling was so strong I had to go home.

The owners had told us about noises in the night and lights going on and off and dark shadows being seen, which normally I would relish and stay the night, but not here for some strange reason.

THE COMFY PEW

My sincere thanks to Judy Leach for this story.

I worked with a man who was a real nice guy he owned the Comfy Pew and did the catering for outside functions from there, as well as running the restaurant he was the holder of a contract for the meals at the Masons in Cross Keys Lane. I worked as a silver service waitress on a casual basis for this man, so you now can understand why I had access to both the Masonic Lodge and the Comfy Pew. I have always had feelings, ideas, sights, call it what you may. Who am I to say what I thought or, thought I might of might of seen. But I grew up this way, with brothers and sisters who were not the same as me. Anyway this is to tell you about one of the events that happened I was married with three children so I wasn't a silly youngster.

This one day in the summer around 1978-80 having done an outside function we had come back to the Comfy Pew, unloaded the van carried the baker boards etc upstairs. (I need you to understand the layout of the building). As you entered the building from the side door there was a flight of stairs in a walled stairwell going to the first floor, the kitchen for the restaurant was on this floor. You needed to turn left as you arrived at the top of the stairs and walk to the opposite end of where you had come up and turn left again. The stairs in another walled stairwell were here and went above the lower stair well to the second floor where the kitchen for outside functions was situated (they had to be separate kitchens by law). The others were up on the second floor, I was stood at a work surface that faced the wall with the two staircases in. I was cleaning some equipment. In front of me was another work surface. I saw a man come down from the stairs to my right he crossed the room in front of me stopped at the unit in front of me where he picked up a canvas cash bag. He then ran to the stairs to my left and went down to the ground floor. I screamed to my manager "a man's stolen your money!". The man wore a long tweed looking coat, a bit like David Tennant in Dr Who, and a baggy cloth cap and dirty boots; he was scruffy. If he had been picked up by the police I could of identified him in a line up, he was that close to me. Anyway my manager came tearing down the stairs and passed me as he went down to the ground floor. A few minutes later he came back up having checked out all the restaurant, he looked at me and said "It's all locked up no one could come in or go out, and I took the cash bags upstairs to the second floor. I came running down when I heard you scream". I felt like an idiot, but I saw what I saw and responded.

COTTER's BAR SHOE SHOP

This was an article printed in the local newspaper on October 15th 2008:

SPOOKY footsteps are haunting a Gloucester shoe shop.
Sales assistants Heidi Kent and Jane Jones at Cotters Bar in Northgate Street have noticed ghostly goings on in the store.
They have even called in ghost hunter Lyn Cinderey to investigate.
Lyn spent a night in the shop to see if she could find the source of the spooky happenings.

She said: "Heidi and Jane have been experiencing 'strange goings on' for some time now.

"When they go into work some mornings there are shoes and handbags all over the floor in the main shop and in the back staff room. They always tidy up every night before they close up."

The shop workers have also seen the shadow of a man standing by their stockroom door.

Lyn said the ghost hunt had been exciting.

"There were nine of us including myself, Jane and Heidi and we had a very interesting night indeed," she said. "Slippers suddenly appeared on the floor of the staff room at 3am yet they had not been moved all night."

"We heard a creaking noise coming from above us in an upper floor as if someone was walking around up there, yet we knew no one was up there."

"I saw several sparkly lights around the stockroom at the back, and a shadow."

And their ghost hunt proved successful as they managed to get a message from the other side.

"We asked twice if anyone was there and we had a response of a clicking noise in the corner of the room," Lyn added.

Since the vigil all paranormal activity seems to have died down.

But Jane added: "There was definitely something going on that needed researching."

Lyn: on the left an orb on a shoe box just above Jane. At this time we did feel as if someone was in this room with us. I closed my eyes as you can see to concentrate and ask if any 'spirit' person was with us. And it certainly looked as if there was.

Previously I had been invited to look around they shop and other rooms by Heidi and Jane one afternoon, so I took a friend with me, Moira Goddard, and she recorded our events along with Jane, which I very surprisingly picked up that day. I had never been in some parts of this building before.

Two days after I had been in the shop Jane rang me up and said she had reasearched all the names that I had said and that all of them bar one (Simon) had once lived here and were buried here when it was the cemetery of St. John's church, which is directly next to the shop in St John's Lane.

This following information is taken from Eileen Fry's book *Ghost Trails of Gloucester's Past*, I thank Eileen for her permission to print this as it is very relevant to this story.

Long time residents in Gloucester may remember the chemist shop Hamptons. It stood at the corner of St John's Lane on the Worcester Street side. Mr Reg Woolford, the well known local historian, told me at this time it was 47 Northgate Street. The premises of the chemist shop and Halfords, the adjoining bicycle shop, were later demolished and now belong to a building society.

In 1875 a chemist named Yeo Hughes used the premises and the shop remained as a chemist from that time right up until the 1960s.

Mr W.H. Hampton a respected gentleman took over the business in 1904 and served his customers right until 1965. Mr W.H. Hampton was described as a tall man with an upright carriage. He was a steward of Gloucester cathedral, and lived within walking distance of his business in a substantial house at 140 London Road.

In 1960 a young lady, then known as Bobby Winter, began work as an assistant in the chemist shop. One day Bobby had to go to the top of the building, where to her amazement she encountered the apparition of a young man dressed as if from another age. He appeared to her to be wearing what she could only describe as a ruff collar on his white shirt and black baggy trousers. He was not menacing, but he certainly startled the young girl. Not wishing to appear foolish the assistant carefully chose her words as she described the man to the other staff working there. They were amused and said that they too had seen the same spectre. Years later she can still describe the unusual occurrence to her daughters.

This incident took place right next to Halford's bicycle shop which is where a Mr Howells had a frightening experience when he was fourteen-years-old and a new employee of the cycle shop.

The unsuspecting lad went down the steps leading to the cellar where spare parts were stored and encountered on the stairs what he described as a grey solid mass about seven feet tall and three feet wide swirling about. Frightened and bewildered he ran up the stairs forgetting completely what he had been sent for and panted out his experiance to the owner. The man was understanding but curious for when he went down the stairs the vision had vanished. All was then forgotten until some months later when the tramlines on the road outside were taken up, and, after a heavy storm, arriving to work in the morning, the owner discovered on descending the stairs the cellar was damp with rainwater and amongst the debris was a coffin which had come through the wall. At one time a graveyard was on the site of the shops. Perhaps the two incidents were connected. This might also explain why the now Cotter's Bar shoe shop has 'paranormal' activity even today in 2008.

Court House, Painswick and Chavenage House, Tetbury

The ghost of Charles I is said to haunt Court House in Painswick, where he was based when he ordered the Siege of Gloucester in 1643.

The gardens and grounds of the house have also been the location for sightings of ghostly Cavaliers who are thought to be preparing themselves for battle.

Not long after his execution, the headless ghost of the king appeared at Chavenage House near Tetbury, the home of Nathaniel Stephens, one of the county's two members in the House of Commons.

It appears that when Parliament went into recess for Christmas 1648 they were still undecided as to whether King Charles should be put to death or put in prison.

Stephens wasn't sure what to do on his return to the house but was persuaded by a Cromwellian officer to vote for execution.

Just a month later Charles I was beheaded, and four months later Stephen fell ill and died, but not before he had expressed remorse for agreeing to the death of his king.

The mourners at his funeral at Chavenage could not in their wildest dreams have imagined what was to come.

As they assembled before church a coach drew into the courtyard pulled by black horses, the driver was dressed in attire only worn by Charles I, but they did not recognise him at first as his head was not there!

As if this wasn't scary enough, the main door of Chavenage House then opened and out stepped the ghost of Nathaniel Stephens in his shroud and climbed into the coach.

With a whip of the horses the two went off towards the outer gate, but just as they reached it they all disappeared in flames.

CROSS KEYS INN

This sixteenth-century inn is a fantastic timber framed building situated just off Southgate Street into Cross Keys Lane. In the medieval era it was called Scroddelone or Scrudd Lane, meaning shroud or garment, where in the tenth century trades in the lane were of cloth makers.

Apparently a very sinister story of a rather gruesome murder took place here, and has been told many times by past landlords and customers. The tale is of a sailor that fell in love with the landlord's wife on his visits to the inn. He secretly saw his lover while the landlord was visiting nearby inns.

One night the landlord of the inn came back and found the two lovers together. He immediately took an axe and lopped off the sailor's head, then killed his wife and buried them deep in the cellar.

He was then so remorseful of his deed he hung himself after leaving a note of what he had done.

The present owner, Ruth Bourke-Cross and manager, David Fuller moved in at the inn around late 2007. After a short while David told me that he had experienced several different unexplained occurances in and outside the building.

When he has been serving in the bar the pump for the Coca Cola indicates it is empty so he goes down into the cellar to renew it, only to find it indicates it is still full, so he goes back up to the bar, looks at the pump again and it is full. 'Very strange', says David, 'this is happening a lot, almost if someone is playing about with me'.

Things have fallen off the wall or shelves in a bedroom upstairs. Room number 4 is apparently a very active room from time to time where a past landlord 'Charles' has said he has seen what he can only describe as an 'onion seller'. This man has been seen several times by Charles. He believes this may be this sailor returning, looking for his lover.

David has said that one early Friday evening he was getting ready to open the small bar at the other end of the inn when he saw a dark shaped shadow at the glass door, then he heard a knock. It was another ten minutes before he was to open, but decided to take a look at who was knocking. When he opened the door, no one was there. David looked further out into the lane and no one was near the door. He saw a young couple right at the bottom of the lane and asked if they had seen anyone knocking on the door, but they both said no one had passed them for a while.

David was certain he saw and heard someone at this door, and it was not the young couple.

He has not, and will not, ever forget this experience as it left him feeling rather cold and bemused. Was it the sailor returning, or was it another 'spirit' person that has been seen walking from within the inn through a wall which is directly over the trap door that leads to the cellar? Maybe it was the landlord that killed his wife and lover?

This next story is an account of what happened to Bronwyn Burke that lives at the Cross Keys Inn.

It happened on October 31st 2008, Hallowe'en Night. She recalls that she was sleeping, and around 4am all of a sudden the dried flowers that were hanging above her bed – they had been there for about eighteen months quite happily never fallen down, never been unstable – crashed on top of her head. She said she woke up quite terrified like someone had woken her up so early in the morning, only to find no evidence that she could see that someone had moved them, or any wind, and that they had just fallen, which she describes as a very peculiar thing to happen.

Then less than two weeks later she was lying in bed again in a half asleep state and all her makeup that surrounded her sink, and was laid out neatly, crashed into the sink. She decided to leave the room as she felt very uneasy, she didn't feel cold or what many people describe as regards to experiencing a ghost, it was just this sudden feeling that she wasn't the only person in the room, and she needed to leave.

She said she felt so uncomfortable that ever since then, in the room that was at the end of the corridor, she cannot sleep in there. She says she has no idea what it is, maybe it was just herself being over-sensitive but there is something. There may be lots of explanations for this, ie. wind; it could have been anything. However, she feels nothing actually qualifies the reasonable explanations for it. She hopes she will one day be able to go back in this room, but for now she stays out of there.

DEBENHAMS

It was reported in *The Citizen* in August 1965 that beneath the foundations of a building in Gloucester, excavators had discovered a Roman road which had been re-surfaced six times. Upon further investigation, the complete street grid of a Roman town was discovered.

A ten feet deep well was unearthed, and at its very bottom was found the dismembered body of a teenage girl, buried with an assortment of grisly artefacts: a severed right arm, a horse's skull, a pair of antlers, and to seal the whole macabre collection, large stones. The body was not from Roman times, as the burial was on the outside of the city wall, in the Kingsholm area. The skeleton seems to be from the Dark Ages, but how and why she met her death and who threw the remains into the well is a mystery.

DICK WHITTINGTON PUBLIC HOUSE

This fifteenth-century building in Westgate Street was once called St. Nicholas house, probably because it is right next door to St. Nicholas church. It has many 'spooky' stories attached to it. It is now the Dick Whittington public house.

The Black Cat area which was once used as a night club has many reports of a dark figure of a man lurking behind the bar seen by staff while getting ready for opening times, and even in the early hours of the morning while cleaning up after the club is closed. Some staff refused to go down there alone.

Why he is there no one really knows, but he certainly makes his presence known when he does appear.

Around the same area is a story of a young girl that died of the plague in 1604 when a gentleman called John Taylor, an alderman of the city owned the house.

Apparently John Taylor Loved to entertain people in his house and held many dinner parties in an upper room of the building. However, on one such an occasion when there was an outbreak of the plague, John Taylor did not tell his guests, for fear of them not attending his dinner party, that two of his servants had all the symptoms of the plague, but, somehow they found out and they fined him £100 which was a lot of money in those days, and disbarred him from the council. They also boarded up the house. Sadly that was not the end of the story, for a young servant girl was down in the cellar dying of the plague, no one knew she was there and she died a horrible, lonely death. Is it any wonder that the atmosphere in this area has been said to be very depressing and ladies that visit this area (now the ladies' toilets) feel very weepy and sad. Is this ghost of the young girl trying to let people know what happened to her and how very unhappy and lonely she was?

We did an investigation here and all had turns in going into the ladies' toilets and staying there for as long as we could, needless to say it was not long, even for the bravest

of us. Also, three of us went in and stayed in there with just a torch light on, and one of our colleague's face completely distorted and looked really ill – was this the spirit of the poor girl who was left to die a horrible, lonely death here?

No one could stay in here more than ten minutes at a time without feeling very ill and sick.

We also caught several orbs in this area.

While on another night's investigation I was sitting at the bottom of the stairs that led up to the manager's apartments when I heard what I can only describe as distant mumbling and chinking of glasses. I thought the landlord and landlady had visitors and they were having a dinner party and toasting to something or somebody.

I started to go a little further up the stairs to listen more, but felt rather guilty as this as this was their private area and what if someone came out and saw me, how embarrasing that would be so I went back down the stairs and sat quietly at the bottom.

Around 3am there was a knock on the glass fronted back door just down another level from me, it made me jump as I was not expecting anyone at that time of the morning, and to my surprise and shock, it was the landlord and his wife and their children

I opened the door to let them in and said 'Oh I didn't realise you all went out, I thought I heard you upstairs having a dinner party' and I told him what I had heard. He looked at his wife and then back at me and said 'So you have heard it too then.' I said 'What do you mean?' he said. 'No one is up there, only our two cats', he carried on to say, 'we have heard many stories and heard the same things as you described a few times ourselves'.

A cold shiver went down my spine as I realised I may have heard some 'paranormal' activity and even more spine-chilling, what if I had continued further up the stairs, would I have seen a ghost? Was it the ghost of John Taylor still entertaining people? I will never know. Sometimes I wish I had the courage to have gone further and sometimes I am glad I didn't.

Will this always remain a mystery? Who knows, maybe the next paranormal investigation will reveal more.

My sincere thanks to Helen O' Farrell for this story.

I was talking to my friend today about our investigation and her and her family have been regulars at the Dick Whit for years. She has heard stories of workmen in the cellar bar seeing screwdrivers they were using float in mid air and last summer herself and her family were sitting at the front left of the pub and she said there's some steps behind some glass that lead downstairs on the front left of the pub. Her little girl who's only 3 said she saw a little girl sat on those steps. She was quite insistent about it and when they looked there was no one there! That was in broad daylight!

Thursday Feb 5th 2009

I and twenty-two other people did an overnight investigation at the Dick Whittington pub, many thanks to Ed and Amanda that run the pub and let us do this. The night was a fascinating, and also rather bizarre one, where we caught quite a few orbs and a strange mauve light in one of the mirrors in the Black Cat area. Several more pictures were taken of this same area and mirror, yet there was no mauve light on these.

We did a trigger object where upon I placed some flour on the bar, and dropped, very gently, three glass stones into the flour, then took a picture of the stones. My friend Paul Goddard also took a video of the same stones. Everyone went upstairs for a while and when we returned the stones had moved, as you can see from the pictures below.

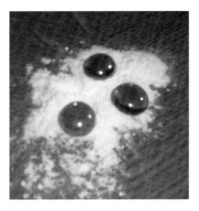

Here is an account given by my friend Miranda Cardew while at the table.

We seemed to contact John through the glass. We asked him if he was looking after Eleanor. The glass moved from one side to the other. Edna said he could be saying yes and no, either he was or wasn't.

I asked if he felt guilty for leaving her down here. Again the glass moved from one side to the other. Colin then said 'it wasn't just you was it?' The glass moved. Colin said it was Eleanor's mother too, the glass moved to indicate yes. I asked if John and Eleanor's mother were having an affair, glass indicated yes. We asked if Eleanor's father was the man behind the bar, looking after Eleanor, glass indicated yes.

Earlier in the evening Darren, Helen and myself had used rods and communicated with this man, dowsing rods indicated he'd died down here at the same time as Eleanor. In a communication with Eleanor, Helen asked if she missed her mother, Eleanor had said no! This was before the glass on the table!

We also did a seance in the front of the bar where everyone present including Ed, the Manager, saw the glass move while we were asking questions. We seemed to have contacted a little boy that took a liking to responding to Paul Goddard's voice. But I had the distinct feeling that the little boy was very young, probably around 6–7 years old. This of course is my own opinion as is a lot of the responses we got, we will always have sceptics and we welcome their opinions as well as believers. No one knows 100% if any investigation and information is accurate until proven otherwise, but that is what the paranormal is all about. Even scientists cannot prove 100% if they are right.

We take our investigations very seriously and respect the 'spirits' that we contact throughout. Several things can be explained most times, whereas some things are not. For instance, I took a picture in the Black Cat bar where I felt very uneasy and in the mirror was a strange mauve or purple shape, yet when taking other pictures of the same mirror there was no purple shape. Strange, but true, as you can see.

On our night Feb 5th, Helen was sat on this table, when she suddenly screamed and jumped off it, clearly very scared and shaken up as she said she saw a man's face staring right at her, very close to her. It took her a while to calm herself down, then said afterwards, well . . . that is why we are here, but it still was very frightening at the time. Miranda's camera was playing up at the strat of the evening too yet it was fully charged. The temperature in that part of the room was changing from cold to hot all night, a lot of people said they felt the sudden change.

Tracy and Jamal Patterson were sat near to the same table as Helen when suddenly the thermometer just shot off the table onto the floor. Both Tracy and Jamal swore they did not touch it, as a few of us saw it fall.

Three different people had all experienced seeing a man's face in the mirror while trying an experiment called scrying, they all describe him exactly the same, even though each one did the experiment at seperate times and had not told each other what they saw until the end of the evening.

They said the man looked as if he had a dirty face like a chimney sweeper and had a large beard, was this John Taylor again? Or the spirit of the man that has been known to haunt behind the bar at the Black Cat cellar bar. Or yet another 'unknown' spirit.

Edna and colin Applegate both felt very strongly about a presence behind the bar where the dark shadow has been seen many times by previous owners and staff and Edna said she felt rather dizzy and drained at one point.

James felt as if his heart was racing in the same area and he felt hot and cold shivers going down his spine. When James told Paul about this activity by the bar, Paul came and filmed around it, and caught an orb behind James.

It was a highly active night for most of us. Paranormal? What do you think? Can so many people be wrong? In my opinion, no, they are all very sensible people and highly trustworthy.

I know that a lot of people when seeing these 'orbs' are going to disagree with me and that's fine, everyone has the right to their own opinions. Here are some peoples' opinions on orbs:

'The term orb describes unexpected, typically circular artifacts in photographs. Sometimes the artifact leaves a trail, indicating motion.'

'The technical photographic term for the occurrence of orbs, especially pronounced in modern ultra-compact cameras, is orb backscatter or near-camera reflection.'

'Orbs are usually circular balls of light. Most are usually white orbs though often orbs are red and many other colours. Some orbs appear to have images and faces within them. The orb can be a paranormal phenomenon but most of the orbs caught on cameras may have an earthly explanation.'

What is the cause of real orbs?

One popular orbs theory is that the orb is the energy being transferred from a source such as power lines, heat, batteries and so on. Energy like a globule of water in zero gravity is drawn together to form a sphere. Orbs may also have something to do with human bio energy and may be an effect of the energy of the aura. I have certainly seen orbs around people's heads when I am making a spirit link. There is one instance that I have described in detail in my book *Protecting the Soul* in which Jane and I saw a brilliant ball of light – an orb about the size of a football – appear in the middle of the room. It was astonishing and in this instance we believe that it may have been a protective spirit. The difference between this spirit light phenomena and orbs caught on camera is that spirit lights can be seen with the naked eye and by everyone present.

The revolution in digital imaging has brought about another far more intriguing revolution within the field of paranormal research and investigation.

Since the mid-1990s, we have seen a huge increase in the number of digital cameras and a range of 'nightvision' video cameras developed by Sony. Paranormal investigators using these new tools started to notice a phenomenon almost unknown on images taken on film cameras and conventionally lit video footage, they christened this new phenomenon the 'ORB'.

In the past three years we have seen literally thousands of these orbs and many paranormal investigators claim that they are 'The first stage of a ghost manifestation', others claim that the orbs are images of the ghostly spirits themselves and can see faces within them. It is even said that the orbs exhibit intelligence and they have been captured moving in a controlled manner.

Orbs around the bar

Para. Science has also observed and recorded these orbs and over the past five years have extensively studied the phenomenon in order to try and understand exactly what it is that they represent. Are they the ghostly forms of the dead revealed with the help of modern technology or are they something much less paranormal but nonetheless intriguing? The truth lies somewhere in between and we hope that as a result of our own and others careful research and good experimentation it is possible to solve some of the riddles and mystique that surround this frequently observed anomaly.

So there you have it. Real or not real? You have to decide yourselves. Paranormal or not? I and many others will keep on trying to prove 100% that orbs, ghosts, spirits etc, do exist and have done for thousands of years.

But at the same time, I often wonder are we really meant to know everything? Again, a matter of opinion.

FLEECE HOTEL

The fleece hotel has a story attached to it about a 'lady in blue'. This was in the 1960s, when she was 'allegedly' a regular visitor seen by two night porters. The two men both gave the same description of a small lady, elegantly dressed in a blue dress with a ruff and flat cloth head-dress. She always appeared after midnight walking along the corridors. The porters were a little frightened of her, but she did not seem to be aware of them, she seemed preoccupied with her nightly walk.

There was a gentleman's club next door to the Fleece Hotel in the nineteenth century, a place where men only could enjoy a drink and a smoke in peace, away from the ladies.

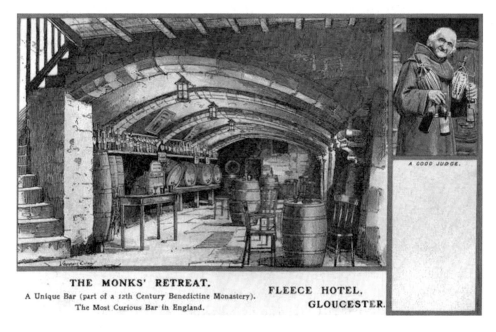

THE MONKS' RETREAT.
A Unique Bar (part of a 12th Century Benedictine Monastery).
The Most Curious Bar in England.

FLEECE HOTEL,
GLOUCESTER.

A GOOD JUDGE.

The Monks Retreat, a twelfth-century tunnel-vaulted undercroft. This lies beneath The Fleece hotel and was once used as a public bar

When alterations were made to the Fleece Hotel, a small door leading from the hotel into the gentleman's club was discovered.

There was also a beautiful Queen Anne fireplace, later discovered, that was also investigated.

Behind it led to bedroom 4, close to the spot where the two night porters had seen the ' lady in blue'.

Above this place there had once been a smaller attic bedroom. The conclusion of the investigation was that the lady in blue had once worked and lived in the hotel using the attic room as her own place.

Fountain Inn

In the seventeenth-century Fountain Inn, which at that time belonged to the Dean and Chapter, was the scene of many a pleasant evening. It was used by vergers, lay-clerks and other cathedral officers. One of its most regular customers was a gentleman called Stephen Jefferies, who was an organist and choir master. He was a real character, and well-known for speaking his mind.

He was playing one day for a visiting singer, and the visitor sang a wrong note. Jefferies, instead of covering up the mistake, turned to the choir and congregation and called out 'He can't sing it!'

Anna Jefferies, the long-suffering wife of the choir master, was equally forthright in her way of dealing with people. She grew tired of her husband's frequent visits to the Fountain, and decided to teach him a lesson.

One night she persuaded a gentleman friend to dress up in a sheet and to carry a candle and a lantern. She knew that her husband had to pass through the cloisters on his way home, and it was here that she arranged for the spectre to leap out on its unsuspecting victim. Alcohol must have given Stephen false courage, however, for his only reaction on being confronted by this ghoul from the depths of Hell was to turn and say "I thought all you spirits had been a-bed before this time!" Needless to say, he had not been fooled by the 'ghost'.

GLOUCESTER CATHEDRAL

This story was told to me by Mr David Leach.

At the tender age of 16 David Leach was head boy at King's School, Gloucester in the early 1950s. He was helping to catalogue the books in the cathedral library one day, and he had to ask for the key to the library from Mr Moody, the Head Verger, as he knew he was the only one in there at the time.

Suddenly David heard a very deep base like voice saying ' When are you going to leave?' At first he paid no attention to it, then he heard the voice again, 'When are you going to leave?' That was it, he answered back, 'I'm going now' and hurriedly left the room.

He found out later that the library was once the mortuary for the monks. Mr Leach said he does not believe in ghosts but he cannot explain what or who he heard, and he has never forgotten that day or that voice.

THE CATHEDRAL GHOST AT GLOUCESTER
by Jessie Adelaide Middleton

The name of Miss Agnes Weston is known and honoured wherever the British flag waves, for her life-work among our sailors. Not only has she established Sailors' Rests at Devonport and Portsmouth, but, assisted by a brave band of helpers, she has toiled for many years—more than forty—personally among the men, speaking, organizing, lending a helping hand, making tiring efforts that have borne noble fruit. No wonder the bluejackets affectionately call her 'the mother of the navy.'

Hearing that Miss Weston had had a strange experience when playing the organ in Gloucester Cathedral, I wrote asking her if she would very kindly give me particulars.

She answered promptly and courteously, saying, 'I am sending you a book which will give you an account of my experience with the Crusader. I fear that it will not be of much use, but such as it is, it is heartily at your service.'

The book was one written by herself, *My Life Among the Bluejackets* (James Nisbet). It has gone into twelve editions, which is not to be wondered at, for it is one of the most fascinating books I have ever read. On page __ is the episode of the Crusader, which, with Miss Weston's kind permission, I reproduce here.

After leaving school Miss Weston took up the organ and became a pupil of the celebrated organist and composer, Dr. S.S. Wesley, of Gloucester Cathedral. She worked hard, practising five hours a day, and during her studies the following incident happened, which made a great impression on Miss Weston and which she has rightly thought worth recording.

'Having to practise for so many hours, I was frequently in the cathedral after dark, the only lights being in the organ-loft, and my own lantern by which to get out of the building. There were many ghost stories connected with the cathedral, and one was the story of a warrior—I think a Crusader—who was buried under the organ-loft. The story was that he frequently appeared, always after dark, and walked down the nave, his mailed feet and spurs being plainly heard on the pavement, walking to the west end: he would return up one of the side aisles, and his footsteps would suddenly cease at the little chapel where his grave stood.

'I had heard all this and many other stories from my fellow-pupils, but I hope that natural pluck and, above all, trust in God, kept me calm. However, I was to be tested, as the sequel will show. One evening Dr. Wesley was giving me a lesson in the cathedral after dark. In the feeble glimmer of the lamps in the organ-loft, the great columns of the nave looked vast, black and mysterious indeed. I was studying a difficult piece of music with him, when a messenger arrived to say that a musical friend was waiting at his house on important business.

'Would you allow me to go for a few minutes,' he said, 'while you practise that piece? I shall soon return,' adding, as he went down the stairs, 'I hope you will not mind my locking you in the cathedral. We are not allowed to leave the doors unfastened!'

Despising, as I did, all supernatural fears, I replied laughing, 'Oh, no! I have plenty to do. Lock me in by all means,' and I went on diligently studying the difficult music, without giving any thought to 'spooks,' even if they had hailed back to the Crusader.

At once I heard a muffled footstep, and the organ-blower came out, white and trembling: he had heard it too. We listened. The footsteps, evidently mailed and with spurs on, became more and more distant and almost died away. But presently we heard them returning, from the west end of the building. They approached nearer and nearer, until they paused in the side chapel, at the foot of the organ-loft stairs. I must say that I felt my flesh creep and that something supernatural seemed near, but I crushed down my fears and, lantern in hand, rushed down the stairs and saw . . . nothing.

A few minutes later the clash of the keys in the door announced Dr. Wesley's return. After a short time he detected something rather strange about me, and wrung from me the unwilling confession that I had not seen but had heard the ghost.

The story lost nothing, as may be imagined, from the organ-blower, and my fellow-pupils were very much awed and determined never to practise after nightfall in the old building.

Gloucester Docks

The Cursed Ship

Some ships just seem to be cursed with bad luck. In Gloucester docks in 1861 a captain took charge of his first sailing vessel, 48 hours after he took command he died suddenly.

The vessel left Gloucester docks and struck a fishing weir leaving a gash in its hull. It returned to Gloucester for repairs where the vessel suffered a fire which broke out onboard.

After being repaired yet again it set sail only to be collided with another ship. Finally, in 1867 the vessel was again restored and was sold to an American company who sailed it to the south of America and sold it to an American captain in 1872.

It dissappeared at sea and was never seen again.

Once upon a time, a ship crew member noticed a rather dilapidated vessel anchored in Gloucester docks, it looked like it was ready for the knackers yard.

One night he noticed a faint light coming from one of the port holes, so he decided to walk over and have a look.

As he climbed aboard the deserted ship he felt uneasy. He opened the door to the crews cabin and was confronted by a man, he wore a mustard coloured coat and a cap pulled over his eyes, but he was floating 3 feet above the ground, the terrified sailor ran back to his own ship immediately.

The next night he was worried by what he had seen, he had to go back and check it out. He opened the door and no one was there, had someone previously hung themselves? Was he seeing things? He didn't know what to think.

The sailor told his ship mates all about the two nights, and they laughed at him and said to him, 'What ship?' He pointed out to them in the direction he had seen the ship and as he turned there was no ship. And according to his ship mates, there never was. 'Ye been on the rum too much me hearty his ship,' mates roared.

Around 1985 a wooden barque (pronounced bark) from Spain docked in the Reynolds quay near what is know as the 'g' warehouse. (The back of the Mariners church).

The cargo contained, amongst other things, a load of long poles of onions which would last a good housewife long enough until the next visit of the Spanish sailors.

The Spanish sailors were well known for their Mediterranean temperment. They also had a reputation for drinking, fighting, and womanising with their dark eyes and charm.

One night, the reason is not know, two Spaniards fell into a disagreement with other sailors from another visiting vessel.

A violent fight broke out and drink was a main cause of the severity of the quarrel. (No change today then).

Dawn broke out and the grisly sight was seen on the deck of the Spanish ship. Strung up from the yard arm, and swinging by their feet were the bodies of two men.

Their throats had been cut. The drained corpses swayed lifeless in the morning chill. Their blood spilled on the deck. Their unfortunate mates had the unpleasant task of cutting them down.

Sometimes on a misty evening in the quay, the whole area becomes very still. A ghostly wooden barque comes into view and for a fleeting moment the bodies of the two sailors can be seen again hanging from the yard arm.

THE BRIDGE INN / LLANTHONY INN.

Thirsty sailors used to frequent this local inn by the docks after sailing from foreign parts. Their well earned wages were burning a hole in their pockets. This was just the place they needed to quench their thirst.

The inn was always very busy, tales were told, deals struck, and pints downed. It was also notorious for smuggling. A network of tunnels under the ale house provided an ideal escape route as well as places in which to store illegal contraband.

The landlord apparently confused the customs and excise men by having twenty-two different doors in the inn, most of them locked.

In 1974 there was a strange report in *The Citizen* a team of archaeologists working nearby the inn (now closed) were using it's premises as a base and also sleeping there. One night they were woken by loud bangings, crashes, and slamming of doors. Mystified and frightened they sent for the police who gave the place a thorough search but found nothing.

74

Later the premises became a tool-hire firm. One morning the owner and a work colleague arrived for work at 7.30am. Standing together they unlocked the front door only to be startled by the sight of a strange man standing in the doorway, he was perfectly still. Quite without warning he then dissappeared.

The two men rushed forward in case he was an intruder, but the place was deserted. They realised they had seen a ghost.

On another occasion the owner was working late with another colleague they were the only ones in the work room, suddenly they both became aware of a man peering at them, seemingly interested in the work they were doing.

Then he dissappeared as quickly as he arrived. There were also various other reports of bangs, crashes, and doors being opened on their own. Perhaps the smugglers are still around?

GLOUCESTER PRISON

In January 1874 Gloucester prison was the venue for a triple execution. Hanged on that day were Charles Butt, Edwin Bailey, and Anne Barry. The prosecution explained that Butt had shot the woman that was his next door neighbour because she refused to go with him to the Gloucester cheese fair.

Edwin Bailey and Anne Barry were accused of poisoning a child, its mother Miss Susan Jenkins had claimed that Bailey was the father, Bailey had then encouraged his accomplice Anne Barry, who was working as the child's nanny, to poison the child with strychnine.

An inexperienced hangman had not brought enough rope for the dispatch of three, so a prison messenger and ex-seaman was commissioned to make a stretch of sufficient length overnight.

50 people witnessed the gruesome spectacle which took place in the prison yard. Three nooses were strung from a cross beam, and beneath the trap door a deep pit had been excavated. At 8.04am on that cold morning the condemned trio left their cells for the last time.

The ghost of Jenny Godfrey murdered here by a drunken Irishman in the 15th Century when an abbey stood on this site.

Reports of furniture in cell 25 on landing A3 being moved happened over many years. In 1969 the occupant of cell 25 and other prisoners held a seance during which Jenny communicated through an up turned glass. After that pots and pans and books etc were thrown around the cell. And a few days later a disembodied hand had appeared and pointed its index finger straight at the occupant of cell 25.

GREYFRIARS INN

Many thanks to Eileen Fry for this story from her book, *Strange and Ghostly Tales of Historic Gloucester*.

A Guest Outstays His Welcome

Immediately to the left of the church of St Mary de Crypt is the Greyfriars Inn. It is situated in one of the oldest and most historic parts of Gloucester, just by the old stage coach pick up point to Bristol. During Racing Week in Gloucester in the eighteenth century, many of the local inns provided stabling for the horses nearby, and the local taverns would be full of hopeful owners and other race-goers looking forward to a week's holiday.

Near the entrance to the Greyfriars Inn is a deep well, which has been used throughout the ages to provide water for the citizens. It is thought that the site may well have Roman origins, since remains of a tessellated Roman floor were found in the nineteenth century in a nearby building.

To the rear of the inn is a large cellar which was used to store wine, and one of the underground passages which runs below the city leads from here.

Peter Kellard completely rebuilt and refurbished the inn before its re-opening in 1988. Peter and his workmen were in for a lot of surprises.

Strange things began to happen almost the instant they started work, and continue to do so even now. Two of the workmen, Geoffrey Lovett and Graham Kahl, who came from Oxford, were to spend four nights on site. This was for security reasons, as valuable building materials and tools were being used.

The two men set up camp-beds in a corner of what is now the dining room, and having prepared for the evening, set off to sample Gloucester's night life.

They were surprised, on their return, to discover that the lights were on; both were convinced that they had been turned off before their departure, and the only set of keys was in their possession. However, they had been working hard all day, and both were ready for a good night's sleep, so they climbed into bed and thought no more about it.

It was a warm summer evening, and their sleeping bags were cosy, but both men experienced a definite chill, which made them shiver.

They eventually dropped off to sleep, but Geoffrey awoke with a start at 2.30am. The lights were going on and off and a chair next to his bed lifted up from the floor and landed on a glass nearby. He shouted to Graham, but he was still asleep. The next thing he saw was a light fitment on the wall spinning round by itself. He dived under the covers and spent what was left of the night trembling.

The next night, afraid of ridicule, they decided to give it another go. They turned in a little earlier than they had the night before. Again feeling shivery, but tired, they fell asleep. At 2.30am Geoffrey was woken up by the sound of his electric razor buzzing away on

the chair beside him. It was not plugged in to the mains. He shouted at Graham, and in a short while loud noises began to fill the air. The doors at the far end of the room were swinging to and fro. The two men quickly dressed and spent the rest of the night in the van parked outside.

Unable to find accommodation the next night, they again went to the comer and crept into their beds. This time it was the telephone. It rang five times on and off throughout the night, although the number is ex-directory. They got no sleep, so at 6.30am, thoroughly exhausted, they began to get dressed. Suddenly, a wheelbarrow at the far end of the room began to hurtle towards them. They bolted down the stairs and refused to enter the building until the other workers arrived, vowing that they would never spend another night in the place.

Since then, many strange occurrences have been recorded there. A piece of timber has been seen to float around in mid-air. Plates have lifted themselves off the wall. Ghostly whistling has been heard up and down the stairs. Lights go on and off without anyone touching the switches. The telephone still rings, but no one is calling. Glasses have moved on the shelves, and strange, unexplained noises have been heard. The present manager, Philip Stubbs, almost found it too much at first, as he lives in a flat on the premises. Now, though, he has come to terms with his unwelcome guests. He has a dear little dog called Duchess, and many times she has been disturbed by unseen movements, and has rushed around the place howling, although she is usually a very placid animal.

Strangest of all is the way the cutlery keeps moving about upstairs in the dining room. Once the tables were set as normal for diners. The next day, everything had moved to a formerly empty table.

Sometimes, extra spoons appear on tables, having been mysteriously moved from other settings. And yes, true to the form of whatever haunts the Greyfriars Inn the lights still go on and off by themselves.

The inn is certainly an eerie place to visit. Perhaps, if you go there you will find that out for yourself. If you dare.

HARE LANE

On the corner of Hare Lane once stood the premises of Halfords, which was a bicycle shop. It was relied on to get the good folk of Gloucester to work on time, and so a good repair shop was essential.

Fifty three years ago, aged fourteen, Mr Howell started work there as a trainee bicycle mechanic. He was pleased to get the job, as most of the lads of that age loved tinkering around with their bikes, just as today a car engine is a source of pleasure to those with an interest in machines.

A lot of the young Mr Howell's time was spent in the cellar down below the shop. A flight of wooden stairs led to the workshop, which was connected to the network of ancient tunnels leading to the cathedral.

He had not been working there long when he had a terrifying experience. He still remembers the day vividly, as he said that nothing quite like it had ever happened to him before or since.

That day a lot of noise was going on outside, because the tramlines which ran past the shop and on up to the Cross were being dismantled, to make way for the motor cars and the buses, which would in time lead to the humble bicycle losing its popularity. The din outside almost caused the shop to shake, and people stopped to see what was going on.

It happened that a bicycle part was needed from down in the cellar, so the manager, Mr Aycock, asked Howell to nip down and get it for him right away. Howell began to descend the wooden stairs and had almost reached the bottom when he noticed a chill in the atmosphere. He now recalls how strange this was, because outside the day was warm and sunny.

Suddenly, as if coming straight out of the bricks themselves, a grey mist approached him. It was about seven feet high and three feet wide, and almost solid in the middle. It swirled around him and he felt an icy chill which sent a shiver down his spine. He stood, paralysed with fear, immobilised save for his trembling. Then, as quickly as it had appeared, the apparition vanished.

Howell fled upstairs, where the kindly manager could see how upset the young man was. Eventually, after sitting down for a while, he felt more composed. However, it was some time before he could venture down the stairs. To this day he can still remember the terror of that moment.

A very strange thing happened a year later, which might go some way to explaining Mr Howell's experience. After a particularly heavy rainstorm, part of the downstairs wall crumbled and fell in. Amongst the rubble was a coffin, which had burst into the cellar. It transpired that what had been next to the cellar, at the time of Mr Howell's employment, was a graveyard.

HUCCLECOTE
by Kerry Lillywhite

Back in the eighties, we lived in a 1910/1920s house in Hucclecote, Homestead, 3 Conway Road, Hucclecote, Gloucester (it is the road on the corner of the main Hucclecote Road and the pub which used to be The Wagon and Horses).

It was a large black and white gable fronted semi, with a veranda around the front. I suppose I was 7 years old when we moved there, and my sister, Gemma (Gemma Louise

Powell) was 4. As my dad was a builder then, he soon started knocking things about and generally updating the property as I think it may have been empty for a time before we moved there (could have been a probate case). I wonder if it was the building works that 'disturbed' things. I cannot remember definite timescales, although I know the first incident happened not long after we moved in.

I was having recorder lessons at school. It was winter time as it was dark at teatime. I came home from school and left my bag and recorder in the hallway, which was very long. Dad was still at work. Me, my sister Gemma and mum were in the kitchen, when we heard my recorder playing. We immediately said 'Dad's home' (because he used to have YTS lads who were learning the trade, and one of them would do silly things like pick up my recorder if it was lying around and play a tune on it). There was no other telly or radio on in the house so it could not have been that. The three of us heard it. But when we went to the door, no sign of my dad or his workers – they didn't come home for about another half hour. I am not sure what we really thought but must have put it down as 'one of those things'. However, I do remember that the very next day, which was a Saturday, I had gone to a friend's party. I can remember my mum coming to collect me and she said, 'You'll never guess what, me (my mum) and Gemma heard your (mine) guitar playing.' My dad was not at home at the time. When he got home we told him what mum had heard and we got something on the lines of 'don't be stupid' – he really did not believe in anything like this (at the time, I might add)!

3 Conway Road, Hucclecote

Not sure what timescale passed, but I can remember being stood in the hallway on a sunny Saturday morning, again just me, mum and Gemma in the house, when we all heard my organ playing, which was upstairs in my bedroom. What was very strange was around the time of this incident, there had been a children's programme on BBC after school called *The Children of Green Knowe*, about children from years ago who appeared to children from the present day (I suppose as ghosts). It had a distinctive theme tune and it was this tune that was coming from my organ upstairs. I can remember that despite it be during the day, none of us was brave enough to go upstairs to investigate!

The last musical episode was very early on a Sunday morning, when both my mum and me heard an old tin xylophone playing (I think it had actually belonged to my mum when she was younger and my nan had given it to us). Both mum and I assumed that it was Gemma, but when mum went to tell her to be quiet as my dad was still asleep, she found that Gemma was still fast asleep, so it definitely wasn't her!

I can also remember waking up in the middle of the night and seeing an "apparition" of a lady, who was actually a friend of mum's sat on the end of my bed! (the strange thing is though she is still alive today, so I'm not quite sure why I saw a 'ghost' of her on my bed). I looked to the door, which was ajar, and I remember seeing 'my mum holding a baby' (again not sure why) although what is strange is that about 10 years later, my mum had my youngest sister after quite a big age gap, so I don't know if this was a premonition or something?) I was sharing a room with Gemma at the time, and I can remember climbing out of bed, my hand up to my face so I did not have to look at the lady sat on my bed as I walked passed her to the door. Mum and dad's room was next door to ours, so I ran in and told mum to "quick go and get Gemma because there was a ghost sat on my bed, to which mum said "Oh, Gemma will be alright" because she was too scared to go in there!

Again, my dad would not listen to any of this nonsense, until one evening, whilst they were lying in bed watching the television, they both saw a little girl, about 6 years of age, walk from the hallway to the end of their bed, turn around and walk back out again. They apparently both looked at each other, as much to say 'did you see that?' and when my dad immediately jumped out of bed to follow her, she had vanished. We were both fast asleep. Dad knew from that night that we weren't making it up and I am glad he saw something because it does make you question your experiences and whether you have been imagining it.

We did find an old, lead painted wooden skittle behind the old fireplace in my bedroom. Dad wonders whether the young girl had lived at the house and died while she was young. We moved not long after that (not because of what had happened, just because the house as a project was finished and it was time to renovate another house)!

I would love to have researched this property to see if there had been a young girl who had died there. I would also love to know if the subsequent owners have had any strange goings on but I am not sure they would be too happy if you contacted them saying basically, I think your house is haunted!

There were too many things that happened there to be easily explained - although it happened over twenty years ago, we still talk about it. Although I can tell when you tell other people about it they are probably thinking, 'yeah, right'. But we know that there WAS something although we probably will never know for definite what!

KIM THE APPRENTICE

Kim Martyn Goodey told us he was not much of a story teller, but he felt other people in Gloucester might like to hear of his experience.

In 1975 Kim was an apprentice carpenter in Gloucester. He was keen to learn his trade, and like most apprentices at that time if there was a boring routine job to do, it was the apprentice who drew the short straw. Above the workshop where he was learning his trade was another small business. A man working alone made his living by selling disco equipment. As one can imagine there was always music with a strong beat pounding out from above the room where Kim was working.

One evening about 7pm the man was working on a speaker. The job was going quite well and when he had finished he began to tidy up. He looked up and at the top of the stairs there stood the ghost of a woman watching him. He was so frightened by the apparition, he ran straight out of the room, down the stairs, and rushed to the nearest church. He told the vicar begging him to do something about it.

The vicar, seeing the genuine distress of the man, left his church and returned with him to his small one-room workshop. All was quiet and nothing strange happened. The vicar said prayers, and sprinkled holy water hoping to put the troubled spirit to rest. The experience was too much for the man who packed up his disco equipment and left hoping to relocate the workshop.

The empty room was then taken over by the carpenters. Now they had the two rooms, so Kim as apprentice was given the job of painting the vacant room. He put on his overalls, put the ten litre paint pot squarely on the strong table and set to work. In the corner of the room left behind by the previous tenant in haste stood a speaker grille. The room was long and narrow about twelve by forty feet across. Kim began to paint a door with emulsion paint. Suddenly he heard a rumble coming from the far end of the room, Kim looked up and to his amazement saw a grille fly across the room and hit him on the ankle as if someone had thrown it at him from a twenty foot distance. No one else was in the room. This mystified the young apprentice who ran downstairs to tell the boss who did not believe Kim at all. He put it down to the imagination of a teenage boy.

As it was just beginning to get dark the boss said, 'Leave the job and call it a day. Come back in the morning and you can get on with the painting.'

The next morning, not too troubled, Kim returned to the room. He got out the paint tin and placed it firmly on the table. He turned round and began to paint the door. There was a big crash behind him and the four legs of the strong solid table were flat on the floor out sideways. The ten litre paint tin was tipped over and the mess was horrendous. Kim said it was just as if someone had grabbed the legs sideways and pulled them hard. A task which would have confounded even the strongest of men. Paint was everywhere and again Kim ran down the stairs to tell his boss who thought he was just covering his tracks with a crazy excuse. The puzzled apprentice then got on with cleaning up the spilled paint.

From that day a series of mysterious occurrences took place. Almost every day for a week strange happenings would surprise the boy. Another morning Kim was sweeping up the sawdust after completing a job, when a large street map of London flew across the room from the bench. It seems that sometimes a poltergeist will manifest itself on young people who it seems are more susceptible to these things. Wishing to find out more about the place where they were working, and wondering about its previous history, the men made enquiries and discovered that sometime in the past, possibly the eighteenth century, there had been a fire and the house on the premises had been almost destroyed. A mother and two boys had perished. Kim concluded that perhaps the spirit of one of the boys had been his tormentor.

Later the firm moved to larger premises and nothing more seemed to happen. Kim who is now self-employed and is an accomplished carpenter with a good reputation, said that he will never forget the days when he was an apprentice troubled by mysterious events.

The story of Kim and the poltergeist were mentioned in *The Citizen* at that time together with a photograph of the haunted workshop.

Kingsholm Inn

Kingsholm (once known as King's Holme) was used by William the Conqueror in 1085, and it was from here that he gave the orders which resulted in the writing of the Domesday Book.

Henry III, who at the age of ten was proclaimed King of England in Gloucester, and crowned with his mother's bracelet, also had his home in the palace of Kingsholm, so it is an area of great historical interest.

The Romans were responsible for giving us a lot of our current knowledge of the area, since they lived in our city and formed the basis of our present established centre.

In 1987, a large-scale archaeological excavation took place on the Richard Cound BMW site in Kingsholm. It was sponsored by Richard Cound who was excited by the discoveries that were made. The archaeologists did a wonderful job, and during the six weeks when it was open to the public, at least 2000 people visited the site, confirming the interest of local people in our history.

Many treasures were found on the site of what was once a Roman fortress. Pottery, bracelets, brooches and coins were among the items on display. The former burial ground contained many Roman remains, including a woman's bone comb which was found underneath the shoulder bone of one of the skeletons. This was to keep her hair in place during the after life.

In the days when Gloucester was known as Glevum, much of the pottery used by the Romans was made locally. A kiln was discovered in the summer of 1987 on the Kingsholm rugby ground, just south of the excavation site; immediately opposite the setting of our next ghost story.

The Kingsholm Inn, famous for its Saturday night sing-songs, is haunted; but not by a Roman phantom, as one might expect. Our ghost is far more up-to-date, if the information given to us by the past landlord, Ray Walker, is to be believed. He has a theory that the place is still visited by a ghostly previous publican.

The first person to experience the strange goings on at the Kingsholm was Morag, the cleaning lady. She was a down-to-earth, chain smoking local who was quite prepared to talk.

Morag told us of the time she was dusting the football trophies on top of the stereo. Poised with duster in hand she heard a click, looked up and saw a large trophy fly up into the air, turn a somersault and then land behind her. She was, to say the least, astounded.

The next strange encounter was when Morag was working alone in the pub at 11 am one morning. She went into the main bar, and saw, standing behind the counter, the apparition of a man waiting as if to serve. The figure then suddenly disappeared. Morag was still trembling when the owners of the pub returned.

On another occasion, whilst working in the bathroom, Morag was carefully hanging clean towels on the rail. She turned round only to find them all strewn across the floor, in a terrible mess.

Wayne, who was staying at the Kingsholm, witnessed a small but nonetheless heavy clock with two cherubs on either side, fly up into the air in front of him. It landed, smashed, on the floor. The clock was repaired, but one day when Mike, the landlord's teenage son, was talking across the landing to his sister, they both saw that same clock fly across between them. It landed, shattered yet again. This time the clock was replaced on the shelf, but not repaired.

Mike has also seen the ghost of the inn. He went one night into the lounge bar to get a spirit for a customer's drink, looking into the mirror above the bar, he saw, standing in corner of the room, a man with silver armbands on his white shirtsleeves. He turned round, but the man was gone.

Ham, the jovial landlord, told us about a large empty glass jar which was smashed in the cellar. He heard the noise, but had to unlock the deserted cellar door before he could clear up the broken glass. He also spoke of the time when a hi-fi speaker fell, completely without warning, onto his head. We asked him his reaction to this, but he declined to comment.

But those are not the only bizarre things that have happened at the Kingsholm Inn. A kettle has switched itself on. A television changes channels for no apparent reason. Electricity is a source of energy which seems to promote the paranormal, and it is well-known that poltergeists are drawn to electrical installations.

A young painter had a frightening experience when working in the gents toilet. He was busy with the paintbrush when he felt a firm push on the door, as if someone was desperately trying to get in. "Hang on a minute!" he called out, and putting down the brush, he opened the door. Imagine his surprise to find no one about; there had been no time for anyone to run away, and why should they anyway? After all, the pub was closed. 'Get me a strong cup of tea!' he pleaded, as he sat down on a chair. He must have been disturbed to make such a request in a pub!

LARKHAM PLACE, MATSON LANE

My friend Denise Badham lives at Larkham Place on the Matson Lane just down the road from Selwyn House and the Ramada Country Club. We took some photographs outside in Denise's garden and orbs can clearly be seen. There is no explanation for these at all, and it was not lights from any neighbours' gardens. Apparently there was a battle at Sneedhams Green in the same area as Denise's house. I wonder if there is a connection.

LLANTHONY PRIORY

One hot Sunday afternoon in July, an officer of Gloucester City Council was visiting the site of Llanthony Priory. The monastic order there dates back to 1136, and was founded by Milo of Gloucester. It was known as Llanthony Secunda; Llanthony Prima was in Monmouth, but Gloucester became by far the more prosperous of the two. Before the dissolution of the monasteries the Prior of Llanthony had great influence, and at one time it was said that the monastery worked land that should actually have belonged to the local peasants. The monks were rich and powerful, and the monastery at Gloucester became the seventh largest and richest in England.

The site nowadays is being restored by the council and there are still the remains of two medieval buildings, it was to these that the employee of the council made his way that afternoon. He was hot, and only too pleased to take a break after his ride where he met a fellow officer and they began to tour the buildings.

They came to a building with a large arched doorway. The four walls are still there, but sadly the roof has been missing for many years. They went through the archway, and immediately they began to feel decidedly peculiar. He was happily discussing the possible former uses of the building, saying that it could perhaps have been a bakehouse, a brewery or maybe a stable. 'No,' was the reply. 'It was a slaughter house.'

By now he was cold and shivering, despite the hot sunshine. Suddenly, he felt as though he were being whisked through time, and looking into the corner of the room saw a huddled group of women and children, their image diffracted, as though they were a black and white photo superimposed on a colour background. The air was damp and sinister, and he could see their dark sack-cloth hoods, pulled over their hidden faces as if to protect themselves as they cowered, terrified, in the corner.

Later, the officer explained what he had felt and it was speculated that the vision might have been a group of Dutch prisoners of war who were kept there for a time in 1781. They had also arrived in July, but as they were seamen and Phil had seen women and children, it seems unlikely that there is any connection between the two.

However, a more plausible explanation has come to light. Before the Dissolution of the Monasteries, people who were destitute came to Llanthony Priory for refuge. It was often the case for women who had lost their husbands and had no money to feed their children. The priory was one of the only places they could go, because if they couldn't pay their poll tax they were forced to wear a small badge with the letter 'P' on it, and were whipped out of town by the sheriff. Perhaps they witnessed a scene from the unhappy times after the monasteries had been ransacked, and the women had reached the priory only to discover that all the monks had gone, taking with them their last chance of being saved.

As an interesting epilogue to this story, was a return visit to the very same site two days after his experience. Once again the day was warm and sunny and he was accompanied by an office colleague, but on this occasion he was physically unable to enter the building. His colleague was astonished to see the hair on the back of his head actually standing out with fear. Further attempts to coax him back into the building have been made; as yet, none have succeeded.

MATSON HOUSE

My sincere thanks to Mark Rodway for this story and pictures.

THE GREY LADY

In the early 1970s a group of youths were loitering outside St Catherine's church late at night, some being lads decided to go into the church grounds because there was a cellar at the back, one of the lads looked up, standing between the gravestones a figure stood out, dressed in grey or blue clothing (presumed at the time) and started walking towards the lads. One cried out, and all of the youths ran back to the front of the church with the figure in pursuit they then ran down the steps back on to the Matson Lane. One of the boys looked back and the figure was standing at the top of the steps, the youths then ran down the lane.

St. Catherine's church

A few nights after, the youths decided to tell older ones about their experience, so a group of these older lads went up to the church and decided to investigate what the younger lads had told them. As they started to climb the steps to the church the figure appeared from behind the church and began chasing the lads down but stopped abruptly half way down the lane. As they stopped running they looked around to find the figure had vanished, so being inquisitive they traced their steps back, one of these boy's found a shoe which was a blue-grey in colour, the shoe was sent to archaeologist who then sent it away for dating. At the time of the find it was noticed that the shoe was in excellent condition but when it arrived for analysing and the container it was in it was found to be in a deteriorated condition, also the shoe had turned brown.

Selwyn House

The results came about that the shoe was carbon dated at around 400 years old, so how could this be? There was never an explanation surrounding this but a story emerged centered around Matson House (Selwyn School) invoving a maid who was brutally murdered in the late 1500s/early 1600s which legend has it stalks the areas of Matson House and St Catherine's church grounds. If walking at night there is an uneasy feeling as you walk between the house and church which is in stark contrast to during the day. Perhaps there is some sort of paranormal activity associated with this area.

MERCER'S ENTRY (PINCHBELLY ALLEY)

This very narrow alleyway is from the 10th century and leads from Westgate Street to Cross Keys Lane. It can be a very spooky alley in the day time as well as at night so I am told. People have walked down here as a short cut but as they get to the narrow end of this alleyway they have felt that they are not alone.

When you consider how long this alleyway has been here and how many hundreds if not thousands of people have walked down here is that not so surprising.

Many people have said that they have felt like someone has pulled their hair or tickled the top of their head or even gently stroked their face, as if only saying hello, not much comfort for those experiencing this while walking alone.

Paranormal groups have walked down here and have captured light anomalise or orbs down this alley on their cameras which is deemed very unusal to capture in an outside area.

On Hallowe'en one year I asked a friend to hide in this alleyway in one of the hidden doorways to jump out onto my party of thirty people that I was taking on a ghost walk.

He waited for me to appear and while he was waiting he heard footsteps coming up the alley on three different occasions each time he looked to see if it was me, and it wasn't.

As I was late getting to this point he was already thinking about moving, but on having heard these loud footsteps coming towards him, and on looking seeing no one there was already terrified himself to move.

When I finally arrived he gave out such a tremendous scream everyone really jumped and was screaming.

When I saw him later he told me his screams were not an act, they were real, he was truly scared.

He has not returned to this alley since.

MIDLAND ROYAL HOTEL, 28 STATION ROAD

Prestigious three-story red bricked hotel opposite the entrance to the old Gloucester Eastgate (Midland Railway) Station. It was built by the Midland Railway in 1898 and housed many famous visitors. In 1979 it was having a facelift to bring it back to its Victorian splendour. However, the railway station had already closed by this time. The Midland and Royal Hotel must have closed soon after. It was converted into office accommodation and renamed Royal House. It has recently been renovated and the once painted-over 'West Country Ales' plaque has been carefully restored.

1902, 1906 Henry J. Radford
1907 W. H. Mackinder
1919 Oliver John Carter
1927 Mrs Nellie Woods
1972 John and Joan Watts
1979 Richard Ray

I have a friend that works as a cleaner here and she has said many times that she has heard footsteps in other rooms yet she knows for a fact that no one else is in the building with her. She has also seen shadows go past her door. The daytime staff have also experienced seeing shadows at the door yet on investigating no one is there.

NELSON STREET

Andy Davies who lives in Nelson Street, and works at the Jarvis Hotel in Matson told me what he has expreienced in his home.

Andy says his son has seen a man with a white beard standing at the top of their stairs, just staring down. While Andy says that things are always going missing, he puts his tools away only to find them missing next time he needs to use them, he looks all over the house for them then suddenly finds them again, but not where he left them.

He says this very often happens. Things are always dissappearing. I told Andy in my opinion that sounded very much like poltergist activity which usually are associated with children.

It suddenly dawned on me that the children from the hotel where Andy works may have taken a shine to him, and maybe followed him home, Andy seemed quite amused at this, but felt better that if it was children then he didn't mind so much.

Will we ever know if it is or not? I really hope so.

NEW COUNTY HOTEL

When we did an investigation here one evening the medium (Ross) from Parasoc Paranormal said he felt that in one of the large function rooms that he could sense a presence of a women crouched in one of the corners of the room holding her head in her hands and screaming, then he saw a horse and carriage which ran over a little boy. On later research that actually did happen in the road outside. Ross was totally unaware of this story.

We also felt that a few of the upper rooms were very depressing and felt that something had happened up there at one time. We could not actually put our fingers as to what exactly, but we did feel cold spots and felt very uneasy.

We asked out downstairs in the large function room, if any spirit person was present and we all heard a definite click or sound coming from the same corner as Ross had seen the lady.

The night porter had told me that he had often seen a dark shadow in the kitchen area, and never stayed in there long on his own.

Also the chef Claire, who is a friend of mine, said she had felt as if she was being watched from the same area.

The New County is now sadly closed, so we may not be able to do another investigation in there again. It is on the site of a much older pub called The Ram Inn.

RAM HOTEL, SOUTHGATE STREET

21 Southgate Street originally and 44 Southgate Street upon renumbering. The Old Ram was a commercial and posting hotel. Billiards were a popular attraction. The building was completely rebuilt in the 1930s.

New County Hotel in the 1950s

NEW INN HOTEL

My sincere thanks to Lorna Hedges for her story.

Well, my name is Lorna Hedges, I am 51 years old and I am a psychic medium, but did not fully understand this 35–40 years ago when my late mother worked as a wine waitress in the New Inn, Gloucester, then known as 'Bernie Inns'.

Myself and my sister went to work with my mum in the school hols, we were not seen by the customers at the times of opening but ended up in the kitchen helping to load the washers.

Mum worked for most part of the time in the gallery bar, if I look hard enough I may find an old photo, the gallery bar was up the stairs, turn left and the door directly opposite the balcony, every morning mum would unlock the door, after locking it up the previous evening, the cleaners only coming to clean in the morning when mum unlocked the door around 10am.

Every morning the same thing, we walked through the door, on the wall to the left were two pictures of monks that were always tilted as we walked in at a very unusual angle, saying this I know that most of the walls were not straight anyway, but this was different as the pictures were straighted up every evening, the door locked, the morning the same.

95

Another time mum stood behind the bar, some glasses came flying off the glass shelf they stood on floating in mid air and placed themselves back on the shelf without dropping, there was a witness sat at the bar but this was a long time ago and I wouldn't know who.

There were other sitings upstairs of ghostly spirits walking through the restaurant. Downstairs was the grill room, as you come down the stairs turn left opposite the stairs, customers and staff often used to talk about the waiter with no legs as if he were floating in mid air.

One of the waitresses had opened up one morning and had just taken the trolley into the restaurant to set the several tables in there, which took around 30–45 minutes every day. She just popped out to use the loo for about 5 minutes and when she returned all the tables were set. There were no other people working in that bar that day.

As a Bernie Inn, all the trainee managers were trained at Gloucester as part of policy, and so they slept at the inn, but there was one particular bedroom right at the top of the inn that those who were brave enough and were in for a bet would sleep at night.

Many of these boys had one to many to drink so they would pluck up Dutch courage.

Another place in Gloucester is the Bell Inn in Southgate Street. Mum worked there when she finished working at the New Inn, around 33–35 years ago. As memory allows I seem to remember one time in particular at the Bell Inn, when mum was pulling a pint one afternoon when the pump three feet away pulled down with no glass there and so beer spilled everywhere, I'm not sure if you know how hard it is to pull a pint you need a lot of pressure, with customers witnessing this event mum had permission to get the newspapers in so *The Citizen* photographer came in to take photos and a short story, oh! forgot to tell you that between the false walls in The Bell people always heard knocking, well in walks the photographer, took the p—s, took some photos put his ear to the wall, looked fairly shocked, didn't say a word and took flight.

When mum said she had a story that wasn't taken as far as I can remember he did not come back to finish it.

OLD BELL

This Grade 1 listed seventeenth-century Jacobean building is in the heart of the city centre in Southgate Street. I have been in this building many, many times on investigations, day or night times.

It is a fascinating place to visit with an abundance of historic tales. As you can see from the pictures I myself have taken, more 'orbs' are caught on camera, and in the very place where the ghost of Elsie has been seen many times coming down the stairs and into the restaurant.

Elsie was named by previous staff that said she was a rather annoying spirit as she was always moving things around after the staff had set the tables in the restaurant. Elsie would change the cutlery over, move chairs from underneath the tables as if someone had just got up from the table.

A past landlady believes it has four or five ghosts, including a cavalier who has stabbed her and mischievous Martha who pinches men's bottoms. I bet they like that!

Dark shadows have been seen coming down the main stairs reported to be Elsie on her rounds.

I myself saw with my own eyes sparkly lights which we call 'spirit lights' coming from a picture frame in the restaurant while I was admiring the picture. Was this Elsie saying hello?

I get the impression that Elsie is not a hostile spirit but does like things done her way, maybe she once worked here.

One night on an investigation I was in the kitchen with a friend and we were both facing the 'in' door to the restaurant used by the waitresses – it had a small window in the door so staff could check their customers were alright in the restaurant – when we both saw a woman's head go by this window. Her hair was tied back into a bun. We both ran out into the restauarant to see where she went, but she had disappeard. We know no other person in our group that night who had their hair in that style.

I bet that place had a few stories to tell also. After Shaun had seen the figure I placed a locked off camera there for the rest of the investigation but sadly nothing was filmed that was out of the ordinary.

We also heard a grunt coming from the restaurant area while we were all looking up the corridor, I would say there was at least five people heard it, so we immediately all went towards the kitchen and stood in there for a while. We did hear a few very faint clicks but could not be sure what or where they came from.

In a top attic room we encountered something very odd, as we entered the room to do our investigation all the lights were on, and the bathroom heater fan was on. We had asked if all the lights could be turned off, to which Nick the manager did so from behind the bar downstairs before we all went upstairs, he told us that once it was turned of at the mains there should not have been any reason why all the lights were on in that room.

We settled down into this area and felt quite comfortable for a while, then in a certain spot one of our colleagues noticed that where she was sat seemed unusually hot especially around her lower back where she gets back pain,she said it felt as if someone was 'healing' her, as it was easing her pain. Another colleague sat there after and commented on the same 'hot spot' when they both moved from that area it was cold.

I pointed out that this was formerley a townhouse of an apothecary (chemist) gentleman called Thomas Yate. Maybe his presence was with us and was doing the 'healing'.

A story told by myself on my ghost walks is one I heard from past owners of this historic inn where a 'ghost' of a man 'haunts' the gentlemen's toilet's. Apparently if he doesn't like the smell, or the colour of the bars of soap that are put in the toliet he will throw it at whoever is in there using the loo.

I always thought this was a made up story to get the 'punters' in until one day when I was talking to some people at the bar, this rather burly gentleman came rushing in after just being in the toilets he was shaking all over, looked white as a sheet and ordered a double whiskey. I asked him what had happened as he looked terrible. He said he would never ever go into that toilet alone again as while he was in there a bar of soap hit him in the back of the head, another in his back, and yet another hit him in the back of his leg. He knew he was the only person in there. Least, he thought he was!

People have reported feeling what they describe as a heavy feeling of anticipation. An old man has been seen in a smoking jacket leaning on the mantle piece in the main bar dressed like a pilgrim or quaker.

The following story is by Lorna Hedges:

Another place in Gloucester is the Bell Inn in Southgate Street.
Mum worked there when she finished working at the New Inn, around 33-35 years ago. As memory allows I seem to remember one time in particular at the Bell Inn, when mum was pulling a pint one afternoon when the pump three feet away pulled down with no glass there and so beer spilled everywhere, I'm not sure if you know how hard it is to pull a pint you need a lot of pressure, with customers witnessing this event mum had permission to get the newspapers in so *The Citizen* photographer came in to take photos and a short story, oh! Forgot to tell you that between the false walls in the Bell people always heard knocking, well in walks the photographer, took the p—s, took some photos put his ear to the wall, looked fairly shocked, didn't say a word and took flight.

When mum said she had a story that wasn't taken as far as I can remember he did not come back to finish it.

OLD CROWN PUBLIC HOUSE

There is a plaque outside the inn stating that in the civil war of Gloucester in 1642 Lieutenant Colonel Edward Massie held his headquaters here. A landlord and his wife experienced some very strange unexplained things and noises here in an upper room.

David Thomas and his wife Jeni worked very hard for two years at the Old Crown, One of David's first jobs was to clean the pipes on the bar, as he was doing this he was startled to hear footsteps approaching the door to the lounge. When he looked up, expecting to see Jeni, the footsteps continued to walk straight passed him, up to the bar and away into the far end of the lounge, where they abruptly stopped.

After having a stiff drink to steady his nerves David made his way slowly into the lounge where he sat down to get his breath back. Jeni was disturbed at the state David was in and suggested that to overcome his fear it would be a good idea for both of them to go upstairs together and make sure nothing untoward was happening.

As they unlocked the doors and stood in the doorway they were overcome with amazment, for there on the floor lay all the curtain ties which had just 10 minutes previously, been firmly in place. This same room was where their dog would not go into. They both looked at each other, neither one of them speaking a word, locked the door and quickly went downstairs. Probably for another stiff drink or two.

Other unexplained things also happened in this building such as a window would open by itself and noises would be heard coming from no where.

In the public room Jeni heard loud scratching noises coming from the pool table area, which made Jeni feel very nervous. It was so loud they hurried up to their flat above and stayed there until the next morning.

Tobacco smoke has been smelt around them, yet they are not smokers. Jeni had felt an unseen hand give her a push down the stairs, and the alarm would go off for no apparent reason.

The regulars have heard some of the strange noises too as if coming through the walls. Jeni and David no longer work in the Old Crown.

I was told by a present regular customer that he had felt someones unseen hands around his throat in the public bar.

Before I knew about this customers story of the hands around his throat, I was taking part in one of Gloucester's old age traditions called the assize of ale, where we dress up in medieval costumes visiting several local pubs tasting the quality of the ale the Mayor and Sheriff of Gloucester and the Town Cryer Alan Myatt with other guests collect money for various different charities on route. Each pub we go in serves us a jug of ale (sometimes two if we're lucky) where upon some of the ale is poured onto a wooden stool where we have an ale conner person who sits on the stool with leathers britches for approximately 3 minutes, if after the three minutes he tries to get up and gets stuck, the the Sheriff of Gloucester says the ale is naff and closes the pub down (which never happens). If however the ale conner gets up from the stool without sticking to it, then the ale is declared of good quality and the pub recieves a certificate of worthyness. All great fun. While the ale conner does his thing, I usually take the opportunity to sit down and watch the proceedings and enjoy a sip of ale (be rude not to wouldn't it) . This one day thou, I was suddenly feeling very hot, and totally uneasy, when I suddenly felt as if something or someone was choking me around my throat. The lady next to me said 'are you alright, you don't look well?' I could barely say no, I don't and told her what was happening, she grabbed my arm and literally pulled me out of the pub. Within minutes I felt like my old self again, and wanted to re-join the others, but she insisted I waited outside for them, and to make sure I never went back in, she stayed with me.

I asked her 'what on earth was all that about?', she would not tell me. All she said was, 'you don't want to know'. I have never sat in that area of the pub since; I have been in there since, but I keep away from that particular area. Maybe one day I will find out what went on in there.

Truly a remarkable place and very well worth an overnight investigation at some point, if we are allowed. The present management are Keith and Geraldine Gair.

Maybe Colonel Massey and his army are still using the Old Crown as their headquaters.

PETER HICKMAN'S

Peter Hickman's is a well established Gloucester hairdressing salon. The building itself, however, is quite old and dates back to pre-Victorian days. It has been used not only as a private residence, but also by a firm of nineteenth-century solicitors. I heard stories of ghostly happenings there.

I heard that there is a very gloomy cellar area with strange doors and mysterious passageways, and it is from this area that a lot of strange tales stem. There is a room in the cellar that is used to store stock. No one enjoys the job of going downstairs alone to fetch a bottle of shampoo or whatever else is needed.

The ghost (or maybe ghosts) downstairs are said to be very noisy, and often, loud conversations can be heard which will suddenly cease as quickly as they begin. Two girls who worked at the salon, said that they had both heard this noisy chattering, and sometimes it seemed that a heated row was taking place. Then there would be silence. They also said that the light would switch on and off by itself in the stockroom.

Emma, a previous hairdresser there, clearly heard her name being called from below one day, so she ran to see who wanted her. She reached the bottom of the stairs, but there was nobody there. Two other employees, also spoke of the noises coming from the cellar. They said that sometimes it sounded as though tins were being rattled about, accompanied by scurrying noises like the sound of someone rushing around. The staff said that strange things had been happening there ever since they could remember. Nobody is surprised by what goes on there any more, and the staff look upon the presence as a friendly one.

A lady who once lived in the flat of the house had apparently seen the figure of a small girl sitting on the stairs, crying. She went to comfort the little girl, but the apparition disappeared.

None of this seems to affect the atmosphere of the house however, as everyone seemed to be very happy and relaxed.

THE PIG INN THE CITY, WESTGATE STREET

This public house used to be called The Lower George, and it is at the bottom end of Westgate Street.

An advertisement in 1873 reads. 'Lower George Hotel, Westgate Street. Proprietor J. Powell. Wines, spirits. Burton and Home brewed ales of excellent quality. Good accommodation for travellers. Beds and sitting rooms on moderate terms, Good stabling and lock up yards and coach horses.' The smell of malted barley and boiling hops must have been quite strong in this area of Westgate Street as the Lower George only a few yards down the road from the Gloucester Brewery which had premises in Quay Street backing onto Westgate Street. The address of the Lower George Hotel is given as 60 Westgate Street in 1919 and 121 Westgate Street on renumbering. The Lower George dates back to the 1500s.

I was told a story of a man that used to drink at the Lower George but worked at the Gloucester Brewery. How it happened no one really knew, but this gentleman had fallen into one of the large boiling hot tubs they used for boiling up the hops, and his ghost has been seen still sat at the bar of the Lower George now called The Pig Inn the City. What a way to go.

John Thorne, was by trade a brewer of who lived in the parish of St. Nicholas. In the year 1595 his son Richard was apprenticed to him and his wife Joan 'in the arte de maultinge et brewing', but we know little about his brewing activities, though one of his workmen, Walter Trigge, was scalded to death by falling into a 'furnace of water' in the brewery.

Was the story that I was told about Walter Trigge?

I spoke to the landlord Martyn Penn in February 2009 regarding any more stories about The Pig Inn the City and he told me that he believes the pub, when it was called the Lower George, to be one of the five oldest in the City of Gloucester dating from 1601.

In the 1800s he said that when the circus came to town the elephants were housed in the back of the pub as it was the only safe and secure place for them. He also told me that The Pig Inn the City (then the Lower George) was an annexe to The New Inn at one stage to accomadate the coaching staff.

A fine old inn it is too and must have quite a few stories to tell. One such recent story told by Martyn was that the gas bottles keep turning off for no apparent reason, he called in an engineer that said he could not explain why this keeps happening as in his opinion it is impossible for it to turn itself off, Martyn says it's always the real ale pump. Maybe the 'spirit' is trying to tell Martyn something, who knows.

Martyn's wife says she has felt cold air round the back of the bar area and also heard footsteps and as she waited for someone to appear, she looked and no one was there, or anywhere near her.

POUNDSTRETCHER, WESTGATE STREET

The Theatre Royal was opened in 1791 in Westgate Street.

When this lovely theatre closed in came other trades and one such trade was a Poundstretcher shop. This is where I first heard the story about Eliza Johnson. A lady in the 1800s who was in love with an actor but he did not reciprocate so she apparently hung herself. From time to time it is said she reappears in the shop and causes mayhem by disturbing stock on the shelves and throwing them on the floor.

THE GHOST IN THE SHOP . . . 2005

After finding the store in a mess one morning staff at Poundstretcher on Eastgate Street examined CCTV footage of the night before. I actually saw the original tape.

What shocked them and myself was the sight of a ghostly figure of a Victorian woman pushing a whole pallet of goods to the ground.

Research shows that the shop stands on the site of an old theatre – The Theatre Royal, later known as The Palace. It was first opened in 1791 and closed in 1922.

It is believed that it is the ghost of the poor woman, Eliza, who staff claim to have captured on camera.

The deputy manageress of Poundstretcher, Sue Cooper, told us it's not the first time she's come into close contact with the apparition. She said, 'You can often feel her presence, sometimes you can feel an icy cold. You can feel a gagging or choking, especially downstairs in the cellar.'

The then manageress Michelle told me that she has often seen 'Eliza' and is very comfortable with her as she feels genuine sorrow for Eliza and Eliza has picked up on this from Michelle.

Staff here do not like going downstairs in the basement areas alone. I once went down into this area, I must say it felt very depressing. Even in the upper floors it felt like the whole building was not happy at all. My friend, who was once the manageress there, said that she had felt Eliza's presence many times and that she was a very sad and lonely spirit.

Sadly we never know the whole truth of the mysterious ghost in the shop as their Head Office declined to allow any paranormal investigations to be conducted. This of course is their prerogative, which I respect.

Ramada Hotel and Country Club

The stories told here are from Andy Davies who has worked at The Ramada Hotel Matson for four years. My sincere thanks to Andy.

When Andy cashes up in the bar at the Ramada Hotel Matson, he often feels as if some one is watching him, not all the time but every now and again which gives him a cold chill. He recalls many stories told here and have experienced some strange things first hand.

He also feels someone watching him as he is locking up at the end of the night which makes him feel very aprehensive as if someone is going to come in and rob him of the night's takings. One Christmas some girls that were staff took lots of pictures around the arts bar area and found lots of orbs on their cameras. Andy says it's usually after 12 midnight when things start to kick off. One night Andy and the bar manager heard screaming sounding from outside, around 2am when they went to take a look no one was there at all.

They also heard screams coming from inside the foyer, so they shut the door and left it as Andy says.

He also says after 12 midnight the temperature drops every now and then. There is also a black Labrador dog that has been seen roaming the area at night by the night porter.

A man in a white suit has been seen on a regular basis walking the same route outside the art bar area. Not just by one person either.

Andy says many people have seen someone walk through the bar area and disappear into the wall.

Horses' hooves and carts have been also been heard going along the front of the building.

One guest was in an old part of the building in room 1 when he came to reception in the middle of the night demanding to be checked out and found another hotel, when asked why he wanted to leave, he replied, 'because I saw Roman soldiers walking above my bed!' The old bar manager slept in the same room one night according to Andy and he too saw the Roman soldiers marching through the room. He saw the full uniforms of the soldiers complete with the red feathers they wore in their helmets.

Andy says he has heard that in the restaurant was a hole in the ground that used to be a well and two children fell down this well and got trapped and died. Screams have been heard around this area.

Also in the restaurant a lady that worked there would be sat talking to people and when asked who she was talking to she said 'I'm talking to my friends here'.

The condiments in the restaurant have been pushed over on the tables and the chairs tipped up away from the tables.

Andy says there has been many strange occurances in the restaurant. I was there on Feb 1st 2009 and took the pictures that you now see with many orbs on them around the areas that Andy has talked about. He was also touched on the shoulder in the kitchen as he was clearing the food from the plates. He says he doesn't believe in ghosts but . . . he also does believe in one way as he has experienced it first hand.

Andy says he spun round one night while cashing up and out the corner of his eye he saw a shadow dissappear from around one of the columns in the bar.

Rob, who works at the hotel, has also experienced things there. He recalls one night as he was clearing up the dishes after a party the doors to the kitchen and from the restaurant when he noticed the door to the restaurant was wide open then suddenly closed right in front of him, he first thought it was a daft but then realised it wasn't as the door wouldn't budge.

Rob also says that someone was staying in the old farmhouse and at 4am in the morning he saw the Roman soldiers in his room, and would not stay in there.

A little girl who was a guest saw another little girl in the games room who she was playing with when she suddenly disappeared and this was in the daytime.

Rob also recalls that 10am the breakfast finishes in the restaurant and the waitress was laying up for the dinner shift when all of a sudden the light fittings which she was nowhere near exploded, and two chairs just fell flat on their back and no one was near them.

Andy also says his house in Nelson Street, Gloucester is also haunted and this will be told later on in the book.

THE REGAL, KING'S SQUARE

The Regal public house in King's Square is said to have been haunted by a ghostly figure drifting across the screen while showing a film when it was a cinema back in 1990s the usherettes said they always felt something very strange while working near the bottom right hand stalls, cleaners did not like to work alone in the cinema and said they had spotted a dark figure sitting alone in the stalls. No one could offer an explanation for this. In August 1951 another story was told connecting to the cinema where it was used sometimes as a theatre for stage performances when a man while using a broom experienced rather oddly that the broom seemed to have a mind of its own and dance across the stage. It was claimed that a spirit was in some way operating the broom as when workmen were excavating the foundations of the building they discovered the remains of a coffin. Apparently the workmen did not reconsecrate the body nor the other bodies that they found they just carried on digging and all the remains were included in the foundations. Apparently there was once a graveyard and St Aldate's church on this site. Were the spirits acting up? Pardon the pun! Spirits of a liquid kind are now being served here, I wonder how many party-goers realise what they are standing on. Or would they even care?

Thanks to Living Gloucester for the following information:

> In 1974 the ABC was converted to three smaller cinemas by EMI, who now owned the building. It became the Cannon in 1988, but when a new multiplex cinema was built beyond the Docks it closed and after many years of standing empty was bought by JD Wetherspoon and refitted as the Regal pub. Where the screen used to be is now a vast area of glass overlooking a courtyard garden, and from the former balcony a stuffed King Kong looms over the drinkers below.

The Regal, later the ABC, then the Canon was the last cinema to be opened in Gloucester, after a 16-year delay.

Construction work began in King's Square in 1939 but was halted by the outbreak of war. When restrictions were lifted in 1955 the plans were updated to include a stage and dressing rooms as well as all the latest technical equipment. Thus the city would have a theatre again, its first since the Hippodrome had closed in 1930. With 1,468 seats and a curved fibrous plaster screen it was opened in 1956 by Janette Scott, star of *Now and Forever*, that night's film. Later that year Danny la Rue made his pantomime debut playing one of the ugly sisters onstage in Cinderella.

In 1960 the large waiting area was converted into a Wimpy bar, and in 1963 the cinema was brought into line with the rest of the chain and renamed the ABC. By this time stage shows were mainly pop concerts and the GODS' annual musical.

Robert Raikes' House

On Monday 12th January 2009 I went into the recently refurbished Robert Raikes' House which is a public house. I was talking to Phil, the new landlord, when I saw out of the corner of my eye a figure walk from an outer doorway into the kitchen doorway.

I was quite surprised as this was only 5.15pm (I looked straight at the clock to verify the time) I asked Phil if he was on his own, and he said yes until six o'clock.

I then asked him if anyone was in the kitchen, he said 'no, why?' I told him what I had seen so he went in and checked, he came out and said no one was in there.

He laughed at me as he said he will only believe in ghosts if he saw one himself, which is a fair comment. Lots of people including my husband Tony think that.

But I know what I saw, and I only had one drink and that was a juice.

Two very good friends of mine, Claire and Garrett who are both very level headed people, one's a chef the other a nurse were in the front room of the pub on Sunday 22nd Feb 2009 when they both heard very distinctively the patter of a dog walking along the main corridor of the pub on the stone floor near the entrance to the building. They both remarked how it sounded like Garrett's dog they both went out to look for the dog and could not see one. They looked in every room and asked every single person in the pub, including my other friend Simon who was working in the bar, if anyone had seen the dog in the pub, but everyone said 'no', they had not seen a dog. Claire says they both heard absolutely as clear as day a dog walk through the passageway. It was unbelievable and quite scary she said.

Services Club

This club I call a building within a building because it is off College Street just before the Cathedral Gates entrance through an archway. You could really miss it as people often do, unless you knew exactly where it was.

This building connects also to a building in Westgate Street (now called the Westgate). I have been in both places and have had a good look around areas that the general public would not see.

I have done an overnight investigation in the Services Club run by Steve and Jean. A very friendly club, it has a skittle alley downstairs which is regularly used and customers have very often seen an elderly man, dressed rather oddly, sitting at the end of the skittle alley as if watching everyone. Maybe he was a regular drinker here?

Upstairs they have a function room where one of the female bar staff will not go on her own, she told me she hates it in this room and feels as if someone is there and it gives her an eerie feeling.

When we did an investigation in this room we did find the room very cold and felt as if we were not alone.

Several of us saw a door that led into a cupboard open then close on its own, right by us.

In a room opposite someone saw a dark figure move across the floor, we all went into this room but saw no one.

We couldn't exactly put our finger on what was going on here but it certainly was something, and being so very close to the cathedral who knows. It certainly needs more investigation.

ST. JOHN'S LANE

Apparently a lot of people have said they feel very uncomfortable walking along this lane even in the day time. As you can see from the picture there is a small 'orb' on the left hand wall and on the right hand side, at the top another larger orb is seen.

Was some 'spirit' around with me while I was taking this photograph?

It is after all a Saxon Lane and the energies of many many people may still be around this historic lane which is off Westgate Street, once a thriving trading area in the Saxon and medieval periods.

One lady told me a story of how she fled in fear while she was walking down the lane on hearing footsteps behind her she looked back yet no one was there, she walked on a little further and heard the footsteps again only this time sounding a lot louder and nearer to her. She turned again and still no one there. She remembers it wasn't even that dark yet, so could see clearly down the lane. On the third time of walking on, she could take no more and ran until she reached going into Westage Street and the safety of other shoppers.

A gentleman called Geoffery J.J. Robertson once worked at *The Citizen* newspaper office in the '50s and '60s and he was known to always smoke a strong smelling cigar as he went to work in the mornings and again when he left work at night, along this lane. To this day strong smelling cigar smoke has been regularly smelt along this lane by various different people, yet when they look around no one is smoking one. It is often smelt in the A.G. Meek's shoe shop along side this lane and when the ladies look to see if anyone is smoking in the shop they find no one is, especially as 2008 the law passed to ban smoking in public places, and they thought they better check.

Maybe Geoffrey is still adamant that he will still smoke his rather pungent cigars despite the law.

ST. MARY DE CRYPT CHURCH

The front entrance to this lovely little city centre church is in Southgate Street and the rear is through an archway into Marylone. Beyond that is the cemetery.

People have said they have seen monks walking around the cemetery and disappearing into the walls of the church, before or after they have been to the Café René is not recorded.

As a Civic Trust member I sometimes volunteer to sit in the church to welcome visitors in the summer months to look around. Sometimes I feel very uneasy as if someone is watching me, or standing behind me, and other times I feel really relaxed and happy.

One summer when I was there I needed the loo so I made sure no one was in the church, shut the door, and proceeded through to the old crypt school room to collect the key to the building directly opposite the school room, on my return I was just replacing the key when suddenly the door conected to the old school room and the church slammed so much so I nearly jumped out of my skin.

I felt very uneasy but went towards the door, opened it, looked into the church, no one about, I called out to make sure, no answer.

I checked the door to see if I could get it to shut with the same sound but nothing happened until I really slammed it hard just as I had heard in moments before.

A cold chill ran through me. Who or what had made that door slam like that? I might add that it was a lovely sunny day, no wind, no drafts anywhere and certainly no one else about. I quickly opened the main front door again and felt a lot easier, but I will never forget that experience and how frightened I was.

ST. MICHAEL'S TOWER

This fifteenth-century tower is all that is left of St Michael's church and is situated in the centre of Gloucester. One part is in Southgate Street and the other part in Eastgate Street.

The story here is of a very disgruntled ghost that haunts the tower maybe because when the church and churchyard were demolished in 1956 a party of men had to dig up the bodies in the cemetery and relocate them somewhere else, but the story told is that one of the men that was on this party said that not all the bodies had

An orb inside St Michael's tower

been dug up, he did not give a reason why, but maybe this is why the 'Tower Ghost' is not very happy.

This tower has some upper rooms above the ceiling that can only be accessed by a little door that leads up some very steep stone steps right to the top of the tower.

Scouts used this at one time for their club house. Also it was used for the tourist information centre where people use to walk right through the two archways.

Then it was closed for over 10 years, recently going to be used by the Gloucester Civic Trust as a fun learning and heritage centre in 2009.

When the Civic Trust knew we could use this building we asked a council workman to go to the top of the tower to take a look at these upper rooms and see what damage or mess that had accumulated over the years by pigeons, etc.

He agreed to do this and a couple of ladies waited downstairs for his return and report.

They suddenly heard this man come running down the stairs screaming out with terror and swore he would never set foot in the tower again, as he was looking around upstairs and suddenly was aware of a dark shape coming towards him, right up to his face staring at him.

He ran out of the tower and has not been seen since.

STARBUCKS, EASTGATE STREET

My sincere thanks to Judy Leach for this story.

During 1967 to 1968 aged around 16–17 years, I worked as a window dresser in a shop called Lewis Separates, towards the end of '68 it became Chelsea Girl. The shop was situated where Starbucks coffee shop is now. The lorry would come about twice a week, park up out side in Eastgate street and deliver clothes on rails and accessories in large wheeled boxes. Once in the shop we had to bring all the empty hangers down from the upstairs storeroom, which was accessed by a flight of stairs on the left hand side at the back of the shop. The new clothes etc, were then put out in the shop, spares were taken upstairs and hung on rails, and the empty hangers were taken away by the lorry.

There was a little staff room at the back of the store room. A lot of my time was spent alone in this large storeroom, it was there that I ironed the clothes before putting them on mannequins in the windows and on displays on the shelves inside the shop. When clothes were sold in the shop the hangers were not offered to the customer as they are today, they were sent upstairs and put on the spare rails. Sometimes the hangers would start swinging madly on their own, as if someone

had pushed them. The rails were around 5ft long, sometimes the hangers swung randomly, sometimes in a sort of domino effect. As if someone had walked the length of the rail, pushing on the hangers as they went by. I was never really too concerned, but it did usually make me jump. Which I used to think was the desired effect required of me, occasionally some handbags would fly off the shelves. Going back to the ironing, I always had to keep monitoring the heat of the iron. If I turned away to hang a garment up or get another, I would often find the heat turned right up. There were quite a number of ruined clothes that I was constantly held accountable for. I only had one experience in the actual shop, this was shared with a woman in her forties she worked there part-time.

First thing on a Monday morning we had to clean the glass shelves of the handbag fixture, they had fluorescent lights behind so used to get pretty dusty. I would stand on a small stepladder and pass the handbags down to Vera she would turn around and place them on the counter behind her. She would dust the bags as I wiped the shelves, then Vera would hand me up the bags and I would put them back onto the clean shelves. In this manner we moved between the length of the shelves and counter with me going up and down as I moved the steps onto the next bit. It was during one of these cleaning days, we had the most strange, feeling and both at the exact same time. We had reached the end of the fixture and Vera was passing me up the last of the bags, she had two or three in her arms. It was as I was putting a bag onto the shelf and Vera was holding out another to me, (i.e. we both had our backs to the counter). We both had the sensation that a figure passed us and taken a bag from behind our backs and moved to the back of the shop. We both turned to look at the same spot at the same time. Vera and I both then said "someone's taken a bag". At the same time I jumped down expecting to see someone. We were totally convinced, but it seems we had felt rather than seen a theft because when we checked there were no customers in the shop and all the handbags were there. The other thing is, there is no exit from the back of the shop, just the door to the stairs, no common thief would of tried to make a getaway from there as there was no place to run.

Waterways Museum

The staff at the Waterways Museum have said they have heard footsteps many times in the upper room, yet they know no one else is in the building with them. A dark shadow has also been seen on the back stairwell. Are the orbs in seen in the photographs this man? One photo taken we saw what looked like a face of a man standing outside looking in the window. There was no one outside.

Gloucester Waterways Museum

Wellesley Street

This is an account of what happened to Rachel Carpenter at 36, Wellesley Street, Gloucester. My sincere thanks to Rachel.

Well, I started noticing things in my home from the age that I can remember (it may have happened before also) is about 5–6 years of age right through until I was 15. It started in my bedroom (front bedroom). Well, what it was, most often when I went to bed and was settling off, then I would have a sensation of someone sat at the bottom of my bed (I actually felt the matress go down). I would look up to see who this was, but didnt see anyone. This happened most bedtimes, and sometimes I would be waiting for it to happen and it did! The strange thing was I was never frightened of this sensation.

I also used to see a man, I would say a bit on the tubby side and not too tall, in my room. He never paid me bad attention, and I never saw him in true form, like me and you, I only saw him as if he were a silhouette, he would be walking around my room with one arm behind his back and picking up things off the floor with the other and then appear to look at the objects he had picked up, and I swear that some of the things that he was looking at were my small toys (little figures). They also went into silhouette too.

The other time, as I was a little older, me and my sister with my friend Claire were in the house. Mum and dad went out to the club, and my sister and Claire went to the off-licence to get some pop and treats. I didn't go, so I was watching TV and I saw an arm come out of the wall and it was beckoning me! Now that frightened me! I ran out the front door and sat on the pavement for them to get back, scared!

When I used to tell my mum and dad these things as a child, they used to chuckle about it and say 'Oh right don't be so soft, the dead won't hurt you, it's the living!' But I knew what I had seen was real and I was telling the truth!

Now I'm older, I don't feel comfortable sleeping in the front bedroom on my own. The strangest thing is, while writing this to you, my body has actually gone all cold and goose bumpy.

THE WESTGATE

January 27th 2009 I and a few friends held an overnight investigation at The Westgate in Westgate Street, as we had heard of strange unexplained things happening there. Things like a door slamming on a regular basis upstairs and yet no one is there on checking. A security door that is constantly locked is often found to be unlocked many times, yet no one has actually unlocked it. The manageress Michala does not like to go into a particular room next to her own bedroom, she cannot put her finger on why, but just hates going into that room, and avoids it if she can. On the investigation we did hear a few strange unexplained noises and we did a small seance where the glass on the table actually moved on its own accord a few times, with everyone's finger off the glass albeit for a few seconds.

The chef says he feels as if he is being watched in the kitchen, all the time.
Miranda in our party that night had got stroked in one of the rooms on the second floor. That was shortly before she and others heard the footsteps above. I was by the door and it happened so I quickly moved, Darren went to the door and the same thing happened to him! Very odd.

We took several pictures in the bar area, in the cellars, and in the upper rooms and caught quite a few orbs on them.

Micky said that she feels that a lady that maybe worked there is constantly turning the lights off around the building, which can be very annoying at times.

On the stairs going up to the toilets, Lee the co-manager, and indeed Micky, do not like going up there on their own, as they feel as if someone or something is always around this area.

Miranda also said that a certain spot in the corner moving around the pillar at the front of the pub earlier, she also saw in one of the upper rooms.

Sarah and myself did not like an old stairwell which had an unusual shaped corner at the top of the stairs on a landing.

The Westgate is truly an amazing place, from the outside it is very modern, but the upper derelict rooms are a different matter and you feel as if you are in another time zone. The old bathrooms and bedrooms have been left, the numbers on the bedroom doors still visible, a reminder that this was once a thriving hotel.

LAMPREY HOTEL, 56 WESTGATE STREET

This was originally the premises of the Gresham Hotel. The Gresham was purchased in 1931 by the Cheltenham Original Brewery. The Lamprey, named after an eel-like fish, was popular in the 1930s with business folk and during the Gloucester Assizes it was packed with members of the legal profession. One of the Lamprey's most popular landlords was George Pugh who arranged an annual collection of toys for children of Standish hospital. In the early 1990s the Lamprey had become a failed disco pub with the main bar only open twice a week. It was taken over by Kayta Newton, a Russian lady, who briefly transformed the pub into a successful Russian themed bar with 16 types of vodka, authentic Russian cuisine and Russian dolls and memorabilia. It was closed down by Whitbread only four weeks after Kayta took it over. Whitbread claimed that the building required extensive electrical re-wiring. The building was boarded up for some time afterwards. It was reopened as the Lamprey Café Bar in June 1998 after extensive refurbishment and a complete change of image. It has since been refurbished again and was called Haus, then The Grill, now The Westgate.

CONCLUSION AND FURTHER READING

Dear Reader,

I do hope you enjoyed my first book. I have tried to be as open-minded as I can as well as being a believer. Some of you may believe, some are sceptics and some remain in the middle (still undecided), or 'on the fence' as we term it.

Paranormal Gloucester: is it? In my own opinion, a most definite yes.

FURTHER READING ON INTERESTING BOOKS ABOUT GLOUCESTER

Ghost Trails of Gloucester's Past – Eileen Fry.
Haunted Gloucester – Eileen Fry and Rosemary Harvey
Strange and Ghostly Tales of Historic Gloucester – Eileen Fry
The Ghost of Gloucestershire – Keith Clark
Historic Gloucester – Philip Moss
The Story of Gloucester – Darrel Kirby